Making an Impact:
Substance Use Treatment
from a Christian Perspective

DOYLE O. WELBORN, MS, LCDC

DEDICATION

To family and friends who are a constant reminder of the support required
for success in any endeavor in life. Thank you!

Introduction

The issue of substance use has persisted throughout history, affecting countless individuals across the globe. This book delves into the complexities of Substance Use Disorder (SUD), providing a comprehensive analysis of the issue and offering practical insights and strategies for treatment. Our approach emphasizes a new method of therapy centered around the individual's relationship with God, the role of counselors, family, and others, and how the individual moves through the process of change during substance abuse treatment.

Designed for substance abuse counselors, educators, ministers, and parents of children struggling with substance abuse, this guide offers tangible solutions to the often abstract nature of substance abuse. Our aim is to encourage exploration, discussion, and implementation of these principles aimed at preventing continued use and relapse into the use of dangerous, harmful, and illegal substances.

Moreover, we provide valuable information to assess the potential of a substance use problem, including common indicators such as tolerance and withdrawal symptoms. We recognize that substance use is a complex issue that affects individuals in different ways and emphasize that there is no one-size-fits-all solution to addressing substance abuse. We acknowledge that individuals may identify specific contributing factors that have led to their behavior, such as environmental stressors, social pressures, or underlying mental health conditions, and addressing these underlying issues is essential to reduce the risk of relapse and promote sustained recovery.

Furthermore, we dispel the misconception that alcohol is less harmful than other drugs simply because it is legal and accepted by society. Both drugs and alcohol can have severe consequences, including addiction, health problems, and even death. Our book focuses on the reality of substance use, regardless of the substance, as the treatment methods for substance use are similar.

We firmly believe that by acknowledging the potential risks and consequences associated with substance use and making informed decisions, individuals can protect their health and well-being. Our book serves as a valuable guide to facilitate behavior change and maintain a sober and fulfilling lifestyle. Drawing on our extensive experience and knowledge in the field of psychology, we provide practical insights and strategies that individuals and professionals can utilize to take important steps towards a healthier and fulfilling life.

Understanding Drugs and Addiction

Definition of Substance Use Disorder

Substance Use Disorder (SUD) is a medical condition that is characterized by a problematic pattern of substance use resulting in significant impairment or distress. This condition involves excessive or problematic consumption of substances such as drugs, alcohol, and prescription medications, and its severity ranges from mild to severe. SUD is diagnosed based on specific criteria, which includes continued substance use despite negative consequences, difficulty in reducing or quitting substance use, and an increased tolerance for the substance. This disorder can have a substantial impact on an individual's physical and mental health, work, relationships, and daily life.

Family life can be profoundly impacted by SUD, creating a plethora of issues and challenges for both the individual with the disorder and their loved ones. One major issue is the strain on relationships due to substance use, which can cause conflict, mistrust, and emotional distance between family members. Communication can break down, and trust can be eroded, leading to further strain on the family dynamic.

Another significant impact is the financial burden that substance use can impose on families. Substance use can be expensive, and many individuals with SUD may resort to criminal activity to support their habit, putting their family's financial stability at risk. Additionally, the individual with SUD may lose their job or be unable to hold down steady employment, leading to financial instability for the entire family.

Ultimately, having a loved one with SUD can take a substantial emotional toll on family members. They may experience feelings of guilt, shame, anger, or fear in response to their loved one's substance use. They may also struggle with feelings of helplessness and a lack of control, as they may feel unable to help their loved one overcome their addiction. This emotional strain can have long-lasting effects on family relationships, and the consequences can be felt for years after the individual with SUD has recovered.

It is crucial to use prescription drugs responsibly and under the guidance of a medical professional to minimize potential negative effects. Misusing drugs, whether legal or illegal, can result in addiction, physical and mental health issues, legal problems, and social and economic problems. It is important to understand the risks associated with drug use and to seek help if drug use becomes problematic.

Furthermore, drug use can have a significant impact on individuals, families, and communities. Substance abuse can lead to a wide range of negative consequences, including impaired judgment, decreased productivity, social isolation, financial problems, and family conflict. It is vital to promote awareness and education about drug use and to provide access to treatment and support for individuals and families affected by substance abuse.

According to Meriam-Webster (2023), a drug is defined as a substance that can lead to addiction, dependence, or a significant alteration in one's state of consciousness. It is worth noting that many illegal drugs have their origins as medicinal compounds and have been used for various purposes throughout history. Some individuals, including Freud, have believed that certain drugs, such as cocaine, possess curative properties. However, it is important to recognize that drug use can have both positive and negative effects on individuals and society.

For the purposes of this discussion, a drug is any chemical substance that alters one's emotional or physical state upon ingestion, inhalation, or injection. This includes both legal and illegal drugs, prescription medications, over-the-counter medications, and herbal supplements.

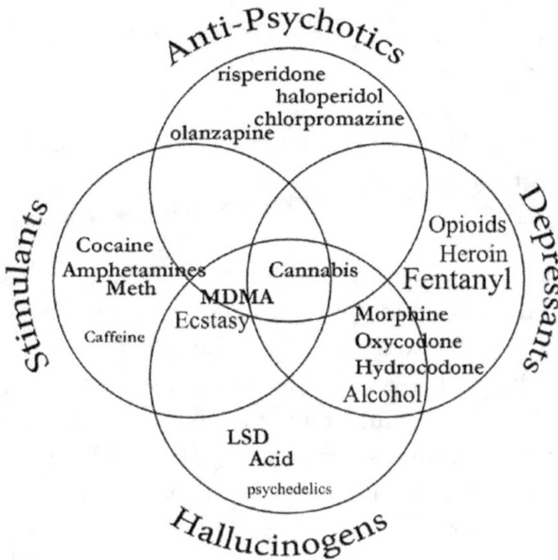

The above illustration provides a brief overview of the perceived social acceptability and seriousness of various drugs arranged according to their classification. Caffeine, a widely consumed stimulant, is considered to be a less severe drug, along with nicotine and alcohol. Prescription opioids and benzodiazepines, which can be highly addictive and have significant health risks, are considered to be more severe. Stimulants like methamphetamine, Adderall, and Ritalin, as well as hallucinogens like LSD, ecstasy, and psilocybin mushrooms, are considered even more serious. Inhalants, such as glue or aerosol sprays, are considered to be relatively serious. Anabolic steroids and illicit opioids, such as heroin or fentanyl, are considered to be the most severe drugs due to their high potential for addiction and health risks. It is important to note that this chart is a generalization and that the severity of drug use can vary depending on a variety of factors, including an individual's unique physiology, personal history, and circumstances of use.

Societal perceptions of drugs and drug use can change over time. For example, marijuana was once widely considered a dangerous drug, but in recent years, it has been legalized for both medicinal and recreational use in many states. On the other hand, substances like opioids, which were once widely prescribed for pain management, are now more heavily regulated due to their highly addictive nature and potential for abuse. It is crucial to stay informed about the potential risks associated with all drugs and to avoid making assumptions based on societal norms or stereotypes.

Furthermore, the medical community has not always had the best interests of their patients in mind when it comes to drug use. For example, it was once common for doctors to recommend alcohol consumption during pregnancy, which we now know can lead to serious health issues for both the mother and the child. As our understanding of the risks associated with drug use evolves, it is important to stay informed and seek out trusted sources of information.

It is also important to understand the specific mechanics of drug use and how they impact the brain and body. All drugs have a specific route of administration, whether it be through ingestion, inhalation, or injection, and this affects the way the drug is absorbed and distributed throughout the body. Once the drug reaches the brain, it interacts with specific receptors and neurotransmitters, leading to changes in mood and behavior. Understanding these mechanisms is crucial in addressing addiction and other issues related to drug use.

Societal perceptions of drug use can change over time, and it is important to stay informed about the potential risks associated with all drugs. It is also crucial to be aware of the potential biases in the medical community and to understand the specific mechanics of drug use in order to effectively address addiction and other related issues.

The Life Problem

As Christians, we recognize that the human condition is shaped by our sinful nature and that we are all in need of redemption and salvation through Christ. We acknowledge that drug use is a widespread issue that affects people from all walks of life and religious backgrounds. While drug use may provide temporary relief from underlying issues such as anxiety, depression, and trauma, it is not a sustainable solution and can lead to addiction and other negative consequences.

As believers, we have a responsibility to care for and support all individuals who are struggling with drug addiction. This can involve providing access to various resources, such as therapy, support groups, and other forms of treatment. It also means extending love and compassion to those who are struggling and helping them find hope and healing in God.

By acknowledging the challenges and struggles that come with being human, we can work towards creating a more supportive and understanding society for those who are struggling with drug addiction. As Jesus said, "I was sick and you visited me, I was in prison and you came to me" (Matthew 25:31-40, ESV). As Christians, we are called to extend grace and mercy to all who are suffering, regardless of their religious beliefs, and to help them find freedom and wholeness in Christ.

Medication Has Limits

Christians understand that addiction is a multifaceted issue that requires a comprehensive approach to recovery. While medication may offer temporary relief from the pain and suffering associated with addiction, it does not address the underlying issues that contribute to addiction. Furthermore, the long-term effects of medication use are not always clear, and there are potential risks associated with over-reliance on medication.

Instead of relying solely on medication, we should consider a variety of recovery approaches, such as therapy, support groups, and lifestyle changes. These strategies can help individuals address the root causes of their addiction and develop the necessary skills to manage their emotions and behaviors in a healthy and productive way. In addition, the support of loved ones, pastors, and healthcare professionals can be crucial in navigating the challenges of recovery and maintaining sobriety.

We must recognize that recovery is not a one-size-fits-all solution, and individual circumstances must be carefully evaluated. While the use of medication as part of a comprehensive recovery plan may be appropriate for some individuals, it should be used in combination with other approaches and under the guidance of a healthcare professional.

As Christians, we believe that our bodies are temples of the Holy Spirit, and we have a responsibility to care for ourselves in a way that honors God. Therefore, we should approach the use of medication and other chemical substances with care, and carefully weigh the potential risks and benefits of any intervention. Ultimately, we should rely on God's guidance and wisdom in making decisions about our health and well-being and seek to honor Him in all that we do. Through Christ, a seemingly hopeless situation can be transformed into a victorious success story.

Hope for the Hopeless

When I was a young Christian, I had a deep love for fishing and enjoyed spending time with my friends doing it. We made unforgettable memories and shared wonderful experiences, but as time passed, our priorities shifted. Alcohol became a regular part of our fishing trips, and it gradually became the main focus of our gatherings, pushing aside the fun and camaraderie we once shared. Before we knew it, we were drinking alone, isolating ourselves from each other, and our bond weakened. What was once a source of joy and friendship turned into a destructive force that divided us.

However, I found hope and a new path for my life through my relationship with Christ. I realized that alcohol wasn't bringing me the fulfillment and satisfaction I desired, and it was pulling me away from my friends and faith. With the help of my Christian community, I was able to break free from alcohol and find new ways to enjoy my passion for fishing. I discovered that true friendship is built on shared values and experiences, not on drinking.

As I focused more on my relationship with God, my friendships became stronger and more meaningful than ever before. I no longer saw alcohol as a source of fun or camaraderie but as a potential source of destruction and division. Through my faith in Christ, I gained a new perspective on life and a new sense of purpose. I learned that I could enjoy my passions and spend time with my friends without the need for alcohol. I'm grateful for the hope and new life that I found in Christ.

As a young man searching for purpose, I was drawn to the "good old boy" lifestyle, thinking it would bring me the acceptance and identity I craved. I believed that being tough and fearless would make me popular and respected, and I eagerly joined a group of older kids who lived this way.

But soon, I realized that my friends were not what they seemed. They just wanted to get high, shoot guns, and drink beer, and I risked my future to fit in. I became addicted to drugs and alcohol as a way to cope with my feelings of rejection and insecurity, but I knew that this wasn't the answer.

I sought a new sense of identity and purpose, one that would bring me genuine acceptance and fulfillment. Through my journey, I discovered God's love and acceptance and found a new home in the Christian community. With the support and guidance of my new friends, I was able to break free from my negative past and embrace a new, healthier way of life.

In Christ, I found the acceptance and love that I had been searching for. I realized that my true identity wasn't in the beer guzzling, country boy lifestyle or the opinions of others but in my relationship with God. I learned that I could be true to myself and make decisions based on what was best for me without feeling the need to conform to others' expectations.

My journey was difficult, but through my faith in God, I discovered a new sense of purpose and direction. I no longer needed beer or drugs or the acceptance of others to feel complete because I knew that my Heavenly Father loved and accepted me.

Treatment Options

There are several treatment options available for individuals struggling with substance use disorder. It's important to note that there is no one-size-fits-all approach to treating substance use disorder, and treatment must be tailored to the individual's specific needs and circumstances. A combination of different treatment options may be most effective for some individuals, and ongoing support is often necessary to maintain recovery. Some of the most common treatment options include:

Behavioral Therapies

Behavioral therapies are a common and effective treatment option for substance use disorder. These therapies focus on identifying and changing problematic behaviors, thoughts, and emotions related to substance use.

Cognitive-Behavioral Therapy

Cognitive-behavioral therapy (CBT) is a therapeutic approach that aims to assist people in modifying negative thought patterns, emotions, and behaviors associated with substance use disorders. The primary objective of CBT is to aid individuals in developing coping mechanisms and strategies to manage cravings, triggers, and other challenges that could trigger relapse.

During CBT, the therapist collaborates with the individual to identify the thoughts and beliefs that contribute to their substance use. This may involve examining the person's history, current situation, and beliefs about themselves and their substance use. Once these thoughts and beliefs are identified, the therapist can assist the individual in developing more positive and constructive ways of thinking.

In addition, CBT emphasizes the development of skills and strategies that help individuals manage their cravings and prevent relapse. This could include learning techniques for coping with stress, regulating negative emotions, and handling difficult situations. The therapist may also help the individual create a relapse prevention plan that outlines specific strategies for avoiding and managing high-risk situations.

CBT is typically a short-term therapy, with sessions lasting approximately an hour. The number of sessions required may vary depending on the individual's unique needs and circumstances. CBT can be administered in a group or individual setting and can be combined with other treatments, such as medication-assisted therapy or support groups.

The Story of John:
He had struggled with substance use disorder for years. He had lost his job, his home, and his relationships due to his addiction, and he felt hopeless and alone. However, one day, John decided to seek help and was referred to a Cognitive-behavioral therapist. Initially, he was skeptical about the effectiveness of therapy but with the help of the therapist, he learned how to reframe his negative thoughts and develop more positive and constructive ways of thinking. John also learned how to manage his cravings and resist the urge to use drugs and alcohol, and over the course of several weeks, his mindset began to shift, and he started to feel more hopeful and in control of his life. With the tools that CBT provided him with, John was able to rebuild his life, get a job, and start to rebuild his relationships with his family and friends. Through CBT, John discovered that he had the power to change his thoughts, emotions, and behaviors and that he could live a happy and fulfilling life without the use of drugs and alcohol.

Contingency Management Therapy

Contingency management therapy (CM) is a form of behavioral therapy that employs positive reinforcement to promote abstinence from substance use. In this approach, individuals receive tangible rewards or incentives for achieving specific goals, such as attending counseling sessions, passing drug tests, or remaining sober for a certain period of time. The rewards are immediately provided to reinforce positive behavior, and they are typically personalized and meaningful to the individual.

Making and IMPACT

The use of positive reinforcement in CM is based on the principles of operant conditioning, which suggest that behavior can be strengthened or weakened based on the consequences that follow. By rewarding individuals for abstaining from substance use, CM aims to increase the likelihood that they will continue to abstain from substance use in the future. CM is often used in conjunction with other treatment options, such as medication-assisted treatment, behavioral therapies, and support groups. It can be delivered in individual or group settings, and the frequency and duration of sessions can vary according to the individual's needs.

Research has demonstrated that CM can be a successful treatment for substance use disorders. It has been shown to enhance abstinence rates, diminish substance use, and improve treatment outcomes. However, the long-term efficacy of CM is still being studied, and implementing the rewards system can present challenges, such as ensuring that rewards are significant to the individual and that the program can sustainably provide them.

Motivational Interviewing

Motivational interviewing (MI) is a form of therapy that aims to help people find the motivation to modify their behavior, including substance use. The primary objective of MI is to help individuals identify their values and objectives, and equip them with the resources and support necessary to make constructive changes in their lives.

MI is based on the premise that people are more likely to modify their behavior if they are motivated to do so and that motivation can be increased by resolving ambivalence and developing confidence in one's ability to change. The therapist collaborates with the person to explore their ambivalence and assist them in identifying why they may want to change their substance use. The therapist utilizes active listening, empathy, and reflective questioning to assist the individual in developing motivation and commitment to change.

MI is a cooperative and non-confrontational approach to therapy, and the therapist collaborates with the person to devise an individualized plan for change. The individual is encouraged to establish goals and take steps to achieve them, with the therapist offering support and guidance throughout the process.

MI is often utilized as a pre-treatment strategy, particularly during the evaluation phase, to assist individuals who may be resistant to treatment or not yet ready to commit to sobriety. It can also be used in combination with other treatment options, such as behavioral therapies, medication-assisted treatment, and support groups.

Family Therapy

Family therapy is a form of therapy that engages the individual in recovery and their family members in the treatment process. The primary objective of family therapy is to help family members comprehend the nature of substance use disorder and develop communication and coping skills that can enhance family functioning. Additionally, family therapy can aid in identifying and addressing family issues that may contribute to the individual's substance use.

Family therapy is commonly administered by a qualified therapist or counselor and can involve individual or group sessions. The therapist may employ a range of techniques to assist family members in identifying and addressing substance use-related issues, including communication skills, problem-solving strategies, and coping skills.

Family therapy can provide a range of benefits for individuals in recovery from substance use disorder. It can help to strengthen family relationships, identify and address underlying family issues, provide support and accountability, and develop coping skills. By involving family members in the treatment process, individuals in recovery can build a stronger support system, enhance family functioning, and lower the risk of relapse. Family therapy can be an effective component of a comprehensive treatment plan for substance use disorder, and since a substance user's love for family is often their primary motivating factor, involving family members can be a powerful tool in promoting successful recovery.

Group Counseling

Group counseling is a form of therapy in which a small group of individuals meet regularly to share their experiences and provide mutual support. Group counseling can be a valuable treatment option for individuals with substance use disorder, as it can provide a sense of community and peer support. The group counseling may be facilitated by a trained therapist or counselor and may involve various treatment techniques, such as cognitive-behavioral therapy (CBT), motivational interviewing (MI), or mindfulness-based therapies.

There are several benefits to group counseling for individuals with substance use disorder. Firstly, group counseling provides peer support, which can be a powerful motivator for change and can provide individuals with a sense of encouragement and validation. Secondly, group counseling allows for social learning opportunities, as individuals can learn from the experiences and insights of others. Thirdly, group counseling can create a sense of accountability within the group, which helps individuals stay committed to positive changes. Finally, group counseling can be a cost-effective option compared to individual therapy, as the therapist's time is divided among the group members.

Group counseling can be an effective component of a comprehensive treatment plan for substance use disorder. It can be used in combination with other treatment options, such as medication-assisted treatment, family therapy, or individual counseling. The objective of group counseling is to provide ongoing support and encouragement to individuals in recovery, and to help them maintain their sobriety and improve their overall quality of life.

Dialectical Behavior Therapy (DBT)

Dialectical Behavior Therapy (DBT) is a type of cognitive-behavioral therapy that was initially developed to treat individuals with borderline personality disorder. However, it has been adapted for use in the treatment of various mental health conditions, including substance use disorder. DBT is based on the idea that individuals with substance use disorder may struggle with regulating their emotions and managing interpersonal relationships, leading to substance use. Thus, DBT aims to help individuals develop skills for regulating emotions, tolerating distress, and managing interpersonal relationships.

DBT consists of several components, including individual therapy, group therapy, skills training, and coaching. In individual therapy, the therapist works with the individual to develop skills for regulating emotions and managing substance use. Group therapy involves individuals in recovery coming together to practice skills and support each other. Skills training focuses on learning specific skills and strategies for managing emotions, relationships, and substance use. Coaching involves providing support and guidance to individuals in recovery outside of therapy sessions.

Making and IMPACT

DBT is a long-term and comprehensive treatment approach that aims to develop lasting skills and strategies for managing substance use disorder. It is designed to help individuals with substance use disorder overcome their difficulties with regulating emotions and managing relationships, leading to a reduction in substance use and an improved quality of life.

Mindfulness-Based Therapies

Mindfulness-based therapies are a set of therapeutic techniques that are centered around the practice of mindfulness, which entails paying attention to the present moment without judgment. These techniques have been adapted for use in the treatment of various mental health conditions, including substance use disorder. The components of mindfulness-based therapies include mindfulness practices, cognitive strategies, behavioral strategies, and acceptance and compassion. Mindfulness practices help individuals to become more aware of their thoughts, feelings, and physical sensations. Cognitive strategies involve becoming more conscious of one's thoughts and beliefs about substance use. Behavioral strategies focus on identifying the triggers and situations that may lead to substance use. Finally, acceptance and compassion help individuals to develop self-compassion and reduce feelings of shame or self-blame. By utilizing these components, individuals can develop a greater sense of awareness and control over their substance use, which can contribute to lasting recovery.

Acceptance and Commitment Therapy (ACT)

Acceptance and Commitment Therapy (ACT) is a form of cognitive-behavioral therapy that focuses on developing psychological flexibility and acceptance in individuals. ACT aims to help individuals identify their values and goals, and learn skills to manage difficult emotions and experiences in a constructive way. The therapy is based on the idea that suffering is a normal part of the human experience, and attempts to avoid or suppress difficult emotions or experiences can lead to increased psychological distress. Instead, ACT helps individuals accept their thoughts and feelings and respond to them in a flexible and adaptive way.

ACT involves several components, including mindfulness techniques to increase awareness of thoughts and feelings and to develop a non-judgmental attitude towards them, identifying personal values and goals to align behavior with them, cognitive diffusion to distance oneself from negative thoughts and feelings, and committed action to develop a plan of action and take steps towards overcoming obstacles that arise.

ACT can be an effective treatment option for individuals with substance use disorder by providing them with skills to manage cravings, stay motivated to maintain sobriety, and improve their overall quality of life.

Behavioral therapies are a commonly used component of comprehensive treatment plans for substance use disorders, often in conjunction with medication-assisted treatment or support groups like AA or NA. These therapies aim to equip individuals with the skills and strategies necessary to sustain recovery and enhance their overall well-being. Empirical studies have demonstrated the effectiveness of behavioral therapies in reducing the frequency and intensity of substance use, improving mental health and overall quality of life, and lowering the likelihood of relapse.

Medications

Pharmacotherapy is an important component in the comprehensive treatment of substance use disorder. Medications are commonly used to manage withdrawal symptoms, reduce cravings, and prevent relapse. The effectiveness of medication in treating substance use disorders varies depending on the substance of abuse. For instance, medications such as methadone, buprenorphine, and naltrexone are commonly used to treat opioid use disorder, while disulfiram, acamprosate, and naltrexone are used for the treatment of alcohol use disorder. Nicotine replacement therapy (NRT), bupropion, and varenicline are commonly used to treat nicotine use disorder. Although there are no specific medications approved for the treatment of stimulant use disorder, medications such as bupropion and naltrexone have shown some effectiveness in reducing cravings and improving treatment outcomes.

Medication-assisted treatment (MAT) is a comprehensive approach to treating substance use disorders that combines medication with behavioral therapies and support. The use of medication in MAT can significantly improve treatment outcomes, particularly when used in combination with other evidence-based therapies. MAT is commonly used in both inpatient and outpatient treatment settings, and has been found to reduce substance use, improve overall quality of life, and reduce the risk of relapse.

Support Groups

Making and IMPACT

Support groups are a widely recognized and effective treatment option for individuals with substance use disorder. They provide a non-judgmental and supportive environment where individuals can connect with others who have shared experiences and develop a sense of community. In this way, support groups can help individuals build a network of peers who can offer encouragement, advice, and empathy.

Alcoholics Anonymous (AA) and Narcotics Anonymous (NA) are among the most well-known support groups for substance use disorder. These groups follow a 12-step model, which involves admitting powerlessness over the substance, acknowledging the need for a higher power, and working towards making amends for past behavior. The 12-step model provides a framework for individuals to work through their addiction and to develop a sense of spiritual connection and community.

However, the effectiveness of support groups in treating substance use disorder remains a topic of debate in the field of psychology. While many individuals have reported success in their recovery through participation in support groups, some researchers argue that the effectiveness of these groups has not been rigorously studied. Additionally, some individuals may not feel comfortable or find support groups to be helpful in their recovery journey.

Support groups should not be considered a substitute for evidence-based treatments, such as medication-assisted treatment and behavioral therapies. Rather, support groups can be used in conjunction with other treatments as part of a comprehensive approach to managing substance use disorder. Ultimately, the decision to participate in a support group should be based on the individual's personal preferences, needs, and treatment goals.

The Story of Jack

He had lost everything to his addiction. He lost his family, his job, and even his freedom. That's right, Jack was locked up behind bars in the big house. But Jack wasn't one to wallow in self-pity. He knew he had messed up and was determined to turn his life around and stay sober.

That's when Jack's friend told him about Alcoholics Anonymous (AA), and Jack thought, "Why not give it a try? What's the worst that could happen?" So, Jack and his friend decided to attend a meeting together. But Jack wasn't sold on the whole 12-step program. He thought, "What's with all this higher power stuff? I'm not exactly a holy roller."

But as Jack continued to attend meetings, he started to see the light. The 12-step model was like a roadmap for him to work through his addiction and find his spiritual groove. The meetings were a safe space for him to share his struggles and hear from others who had been through similar experiences. He even found a sense of community and made new friends!

The best part was that Jack's recovery wasn't just about him. The 12-step model helped him take responsibility for his past actions and make amends with his loved ones. And with the help of his new friends, Jack started to rebuild those relationships he had lost.

Now, Jack wasn't exactly religious, but he did find his own way to spirituality. Jack found people in that group who really cared! His friend in AA encouraged him to attend those meetings, and that was enough true care and concern that Jack needed to see that God was looking out for him.

Thanks to AA, Jack found a group of people who understood him and supported him on his journey towards sobriety. And guess what? He's still sober! He's even become a sponsor to others who are struggling with addiction. Jack knows that the 12-step model was the key to his success, and he's grateful for the support and guidance he received from his friend and the group.

Support for All Users

Support groups are an excellent resource for individuals who are struggling with substance use disorder. Whether they are focused on specific substances or populations, these groups provide a safe space for individuals to connect with others who understand the challenges of addiction. While support groups are not a replacement for professional treatment, they can be a valuable complement to other treatment options, such as medication-assisted treatment and behavioral therapies.

One of the primary benefits of support groups is the emotional support they provide. Individuals in recovery can often feel isolated and misunderstood, but support groups offer a sense of community and camaraderie that can help combat these feelings. Participants can share their stories, challenges, and successes in a non-judgmental environment, which can help to reduce feelings of shame and stigma.

In addition to emotional support, support groups can also offer practical resources and guidance. This can include information on treatment options, tips for managing triggers and cravings, and connections to other resources in the community. For example, a support group for individuals with opioid use disorder may provide information on medication-assisted treatment options like methadone or buprenorphine.

The sense of community and shared experience provided by support groups can be a crucial factor in maintaining sobriety and improving overall quality of life. The encouragement and support provided by other members can help individuals stay motivated and committed to their recovery journey. This is particularly true for Alcoholics Anonymous (AA), which has been successful in helping individuals maintain sobriety for more than 80 years. AA is based on the idea of shared experience and support, and provides a structured approach to recovery through its 12-step program.

Residential Treatment

Residential treatment programs, also known as inpatient programs, provide individuals with a structured environment in which to focus on their recovery. These programs are typically located in a hospital, clinic, or residential facility, and involve a combination of behavioral therapies, group counseling, and medication management.

In residential treatment, individuals live on-site and receive round-the-clock care and support. The programs are typically designed to be intensive and immersive, with a focus on building skills and strategies for managing substance use disorder. Residential treatment programs can vary in length, from a few weeks to several months, depending on the individual's needs and circumstances.

Residential treatment programs may also be available within correctional facilities, such as prisons or jails. These programs are designed to provide treatment for individuals who are incarcerated and struggling with substance use disorder. In-prison treatment programs typically involve a combination of behavioral therapies (especially Cognitive-Behavioral Therapy), group counseling, and medication management, and may be integrated with other services, such as vocational training and education.

Residential treatment programs can be an effective option for individuals with severe substance use disorder or co-occurring mental health conditions. The structured environment can provide individuals with the support and guidance they need to develop the skills and strategies necessary for maintaining sobriety. Residential treatment programs can also provide a break from the stresses and triggers of everyday life, allowing individuals to focus solely on their recovery.

However, residential treatment programs can be expensive and may not be accessible for everyone. In addition, the intensive nature of these programs may not be necessary or appropriate for individuals with milder substance use disorder. It's important for individuals to work with a healthcare provider to determine the most appropriate treatment options based on their individual needs and circumstances.

Outpatient Treatment

Outpatient treatment is a type of treatment for substance use disorder that allows individuals to receive care while living at home or in a sober living environment. Outpatient treatment programs vary in intensity and duration, but they generally involve a combination of behavioral therapies, group counseling, and medication management.

Outpatient treatment can be an effective option for individuals with milder substance use disorder, those with a strong support system, or those who have completed a more intensive treatment program and are looking to transition to a less intensive level of care. Outpatient treatment can also be a more affordable and accessible option than residential treatment.

Outpatient treatment programs can vary in terms of the level of intensity, and the frequency and duration of treatment sessions. Here are some examples of different types of outpatient treatment:

1. Partial hospitalization programs (PHP): PHPs are a more intensive form of outpatient treatment that involves daily treatment sessions at a hospital or clinic. PHPs may be appropriate for individuals who require more structure and support than traditional outpatient programs.

2. Intensive outpatient programs (IOP): IOPs involve multiple treatment sessions per week, typically lasting several hours per session. IOPs can provide a high level of support and structure while allowing individuals to maintain their work or school commitments.

3. Traditional outpatient programs: Traditional outpatient programs may involve weekly or biweekly treatment sessions, typically lasting around an hour per session. These programs can be a good option for individuals with milder substance use disorder or those who have completed a more intensive treatment program.

Outpatient treatment programs can also be delivered in a variety of settings, including community health centers, hospitals, and private practices. Some outpatient treatment programs may also offer telehealth services, allowing individuals to receive care remotely through video or phone appointments. Outpatient treatment programs can be an effective option for individuals with substance use disorder who are motivated to make positive changes in their life and are looking for a flexible and accessible treatment option.

Christian-Based Treatment Options

Christians, like anyone else, may struggle with addiction despite their faith. However, the Christian worldview and beliefs can have unique implications for the treatment process. Because the church is such an essential aspect of the life of many Christians, integrating addiction treatment with spiritual guidance and support can be valuable. While some individual churches may not offer addiction support, many have recognized the need for such assistance and are now providing it.

There are several treatment options available for Christians with substance use disorder that are based on Christian principles and values. These treatments may include the integration of spiritual and religious practices to help individuals in recovery develop a sense of purpose, meaning, and connection to a higher power.

Faith-based counseling is one option. Christian counseling integrates spiritual and religious beliefs into the therapeutic process. Christian counselors can provide guidance and support for individuals in recovery, while also incorporating biblical teachings and principles into the treatment process.

Another option is Christian 12-step programs, such as Celebrate Recovery, which are designed to provide support and guidance for individuals in recovery from substance use disorder. These programs use the same 12-

step model as traditional 12-step programs but incorporate Christian teachings and principles.

Christian rehab centers are treatment centers that incorporate Christian principles and values into the treatment process. These centers offer various treatment options such as individual and group counseling, medication-assisted treatment, and spiritual practices.

Church-based support groups are another option. Many churches offer support groups for individuals in recovery from substance use disorder. These groups may be based on the 12-step model or other Christian-based principles and can provide a sense of community and peer support.

Bible study and prayer can also be incorporated into the treatment process as a way of connecting with a higher power and developing a sense of purpose and meaning. Some treatment programs may offer group or individual Bible study or prayer sessions as part of their treatment options.

It's important to work with a healthcare provider to determine the most appropriate treatment options based on individual needs and circumstances. Christian-based treatment options can be an effective way of integrating spiritual and religious practices into the treatment process while also providing the necessary support and guidance for lasting recovery.

Coping Skills

Defensive Mechanisms

As mental health professionals, it is our responsibility to provide a safe and non-judgmental space for individuals to explore their substance use and work towards building a healthier future. Most individuals immediately become defensive then asked about the reason for behaviors. Being in prison for substance use can be embarrassing, to say the least.

The Story of James

As a former inmate who had been released from prison after serving time for drug-related offenses, James had a wife and two young children who relied on him to provide for them. However, he struggled to find work and make ends meet after his release. The stress of everyday life was lot to handle.

James attended a job fair, hoping to find employment, but his efforts were in vain. No one was willing to hire a convicted felon. He became increasingly desperate and worried about his family's well-being.

One day, James ran into an old friend who offered him a job "distributing" drugs. At first, he resisted the temptation, but he knew that he had to do whatever it takes to support his family. James began selling drugs and making a considerable amount of money.

Despite the risks and the possibility of returning to prison, James continued to sell drugs, believing that it was the only way to provide for his family.

However, it wasn't long before he was caught by the authorities and sent back to prison.

While in prison, James was "voluntold" to attend a substance treatment program. He met with his counselor who asked him why he was incarcerated. James explained that he had turned to drug dealing because he could not find a job to support his family. The counselor listened carefully and suggested that there were other ways to make money without resorting to crime.

With the counselor's help, James was able to enroll in a job training program and learn new skills that would help him find legal employment. He also attended therapy sessions to address the underlying issues that led him to drug dealing. James realized that he had been misguided in his thinking that selling drugs was the only way to provide for his family.

Today, James is a changed man. Free on parole, he now has a stable job and has been able to provide for his family without resorting to crime. He knows that the counselor was right when he suggested that there are other ways to make money without putting himself and his family in danger. James is grateful for the support he received and for the chance to turn his life around.

Ego Defensive Mechanisms

Incarcerated individuals often experience negative peer pressure that may cause them to avoid confessing their guilt due to shame and embarrassment, which can negatively affect their self-esteem. This behavior may be attributed to the ego, which is a key component of the psyche that helps individuals navigate reality by mediating between their internal perceptions and external experiences. The ego functions as a protective shield that allows individuals to manage life's challenges and view themselves as good people. However, when people make mistakes or engage in problematic behaviors, such as substance use, their ego may become bruised, leading to defensive mechanisms such as denial or avoidance.

It is crucial to address defensive mechanisms in a non-judgmental and empathetic manner, especially when it comes to confronting substance use disorder. One way to do this is by acknowledging the validity of the client's perspective and explaining the potential reasons behind their behavior, such as defensive listening. Enabling behaviors, such as providing financial assistance or a place to stay, can ultimately perpetuate an individual's addiction and hinder their ability to make positive changes. It may be necessary to set boundaries and implement tough love to support positive change and promote long-term recovery.

While it is understandable to want to protect our self-image, it is crucial to face the truth about our substance use and seek help when needed. By promoting awareness of the potential motivations behind resistance and the importance of addressing substance use, counselors can help clients and their families make positive changes and overcome addiction. Defensive mechanisms are designed to protect individuals from uncomfortable emotions, such as shame or guilt. However, such defense mechanisms can lead to psychological distress and disorders when individuals are unable to respond appropriately to confrontations. It is necessary to break down these defensive postures in order to identify and address the root cause of substance use disorder. Through the process of uprooting the problem, healing can begin.

The Body's Defenses

The human body has developed various mechanisms to protect itself from foreign substances that can pose a risk to its internal organs. Despite these protective measures, drugs are able to penetrate the body's defenses and reach their intended targets due to their ability to specifically cross these barriers and interact with the body's internal systems. For example, opioids and benzodiazepines can cross the blood-brain barrier and bind to specific receptors in the brain, leading to their psychoactive effects. Some drugs, such as alcohol and certain prescription medications, can also overwhelm the liver's detoxification system, leading to potential liver damage.

Drug refinement has been a continuous process for centuries, with the aim of increasing the potency and effectiveness of drugs. The refinement process has progressed from traditional cultivation methods to more advanced techniques such as hydroponic cultivation, which allows for greater control over the plant's growing conditions and ultimately results in more potent drugs. The refinement of coca leaves into cocaine is another example of drug refinement. Similarly, the transformation of opium into heroin is an example of the refinement process.

Making and IMPACT

While drug refinement has led to more potent and effective drugs, it has also resulted in negative consequences such as increased addiction and drug-related harm. For example, the refinement of opium into heroin has significantly increased its addictive potential and resulted in a higher risk of overdose. The refinement process has also contributed to the emergence of new and more dangerous drugs such as fentanyl, which has a much higher potency than heroin and poses a significant risk of overdose.

The invention of the hypodermic needle is another significant development in the progression of drug refinement. The hypodermic needle allowed drugs to be injected directly into the bloodstream, which increases their potency and addictive potential. The progression of drug refinement and experimentation has resulted in the creation of more potent and addictive drugs, and has contributed to the current drug epidemic that we face today.

Recovery from drug use is a complex and ongoing process that involves addressing physical and psychological effects, making positive lifestyle changes, and finding support from others. The decision to use drugs as a means of achieving happiness represents a deviation from the natural process of emotional development, as it bypasses the more sustainable means of experiencing joy. While drugs may provide temporary feelings of euphoria, they do not address the underlying emotional needs that drive individuals to seek happiness in the first place. In fact, drug use can further exacerbate emotional issues and lead to addiction, negative physical and mental health outcomes, and social and legal consequences.

The over-reliance on drugs to achieve happiness can also have detrimental effects on an individual's overall well-being, both physically and mentally. The use of drugs can lead to a destabilization of the individual's emotional state, causing problems such as depression, anxiety, and addiction. Additionally, drug use can lead to decreased ability to experience pleasure in other aspects of life, ultimately hindering the ability to find happiness through natural means.

Making and IMPACT

Drug use is not a sustainable or healthy way to achieve happiness. Instead, individuals can seek alternative means of achieving happiness such as therapy, exercise, and connecting with friends and loved ones. Recovery from drug use is a process that requires patience, commitment, and support, and taking steps to address underlying emotional needs and make positive lifestyle changes can lead to long-term recovery and a more fulfilling life.

The human brain's reward system is a complex network of structures that plays a critical role in regulating our emotions, motivation, and pleasure. The system is susceptible to manipulation and can be exploited by substances like drugs, leading to addiction. The famous experiment by Olds and Milner in 1954, in which rats could self-stimulate the nucleus accumbens area of the brain and experience intense pleasure, highlights the importance of understanding the brain's reward system and the potential dangers of addiction. While the experiment is not a direct comparison to human behavior and addiction, it provides valuable insights into the underlying mechanisms of pleasure and reward in the brain, emphasizing the need for a better understanding of addiction's complex nature. In this context, drug use and pornography consumption can have detrimental effects on an individual's well-being, as they provide a shortcut to achieving pleasure that can cause the brain to develop a dependence on this shortcut. It is essential to recognize the importance of natural processes, such as social interactions, physical activity, and other activities, to experience pleasure and happiness, rather than relying on these shortcuts.

The brain's reward system plays a crucial role in regulating our emotions, motivation, and pleasure. The pleasure center in the brain is a complex network of structures that includes the nucleus accumbens, the ventral tegmental area, and the prefrontal cortex, among others. These structures work together to create a feedback loop that reinforces behaviors that are associated with pleasure and reward.

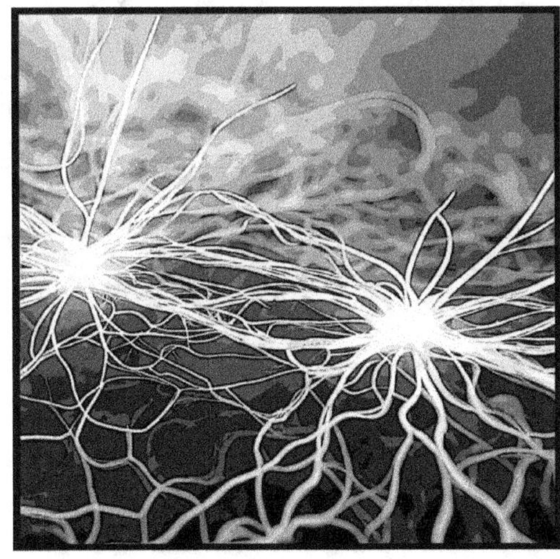

Drug use and pornography consumption are two examples of behaviors that can activate the brain's pleasure center. Research has shown that these activities can release large amounts of dopamine, a neurotransmitter that is involved in feelings of pleasure and reward. This flood of dopamine can create a powerful and intense sensation of pleasure that can be difficult for the brain to ignore.

The potential for addiction is particularly strong when an individual is able to activate the pleasure center easily and frequently. Studies have shown that the same brain regions that are activated by drug use and pornography consumption are also involved in the regulation of natural rewards, such as food and social interaction. This can lead to a "hijacking" of the brain's reward system, where the individual becomes so focused on the short-term pleasure of drug use or pornography that they neglect other essential needs, such as food, water, and relationships.

While the James Olds experiment with rats is not a direct comparison to human behavior and addiction, it does provide an important example of the power and susceptibility of the brain's reward system to manipulation. Further research is needed to better understand the complex nature of addiction, but it is clear that the brain's reward system plays a critical role in the development of addiction and the need for a greater understanding of the mechanisms that underlie addiction.

The ease of access to pornography through the internet has led to an increase in the consumption of sexually explicit content. The brain's reward system is activated by the images and videos, which can lead to the formation of habits and compulsions, similar to drug addiction. This overstimulation of the reward system can lead to the neglect of traditional courtship and commitment in relationships, as well as a decreased ability to experience pleasure in other aspects of life. It is important to understand that pornography consumption can have negative consequences on an individual's physical and mental health, as well as their relationships with others. Seeking out healthy ways to achieve pleasure and happiness is essential for overall well-being.

Similarly, drug use can lead to a disregard for responsibilities and relationships. The use of drugs as a shortcut to pleasure can lead to addiction, physical and mental health issues, and a decreased ability to experience pleasure in other aspects of life. The use of drugs can destabilize an individual's emotional state, leading to problems such as depression, anxiety, and more. It is crucial for individuals to recognize the negative effects of these shortcuts and to seek out healthy ways to achieve pleasure and happiness, such as engaging in meaningful activities, cultivating positive relationships, and finding purpose and meaning in life.

Alternatives to Drug Use

Engaging in intense physical activity and new experiences can have significant impacts on the brain and body by activating similar neurotransmitters as drugs like cocaine and marijuana. Endorphins, one of the neurotransmitters released during intense physical activity, produces feelings of pleasure and reduces pain. Similarly, dopamine is released during new experiences, and it's responsible for feelings of pleasure and reward. These neurotransmitters can lead to feelings of euphoria, joy, and contentment, helping individuals cope with stress and enhance overall well-being.

Not only do these activities provide a natural high similar to drug use, but they also offer additional benefits that drugs cannot provide. Intense physical activity can improve physical health and fitness, while new experiences can broaden horizons, enhance creativity, and foster social connections. These activities can be a healthier and more sustainable way to achieve a sense of euphoria and well-being, without the negative consequences associated with drug abuse.

It's important to note, however, that not all physical activities and new experiences are equally beneficial. Engaging in activities that are enjoyable and meaningful to the individual is essential for reaping the full benefits of the natural high. Furthermore, individuals with preexisting physical or mental health conditions should consult with a healthcare professional before engaging in intense physical activity.

Coping Skills

Prolonged drug use can severely impact an individual's ability to cope with the stresses and challenges of everyday life. By using drugs as a coping mechanism, individuals may find temporary relief from stress and negative emotions. However, this temporary escape is not a sustainable solution, and prolonged drug use can lead to addiction and worsen an individual's ability to cope with stress over time. Additionally, individuals who rely on drugs as a coping mechanism often lack healthy coping mechanisms, leaving them with superficial and temporary solutions that do not address the root cause of the stressor.

Healthy coping mechanisms, on the other hand, are effective in managing stress and improving overall well-being. These can include behaviors such as exercise, meditation, therapy, and social support. Healthy coping mechanisms are more sustainable and provide individuals with the tools they need to manage stress and negative emotions in a healthy and productive way. As individuals grow and learn, they can develop new and more effective coping mechanisms, allowing them to be resilient in the face of future challenges.

While temporary coping mechanisms can provide relief from stress in the short term, it is essential to develop healthy coping mechanisms that address the root cause of the stressor. By relying on healthy coping mechanisms, individuals can effectively manage stress and improve their overall well-being in a sustainable way.

Some Possible Problems with Coping Skills

Apathy, lack of belonging, low self-esteem, discontentment, marriage problems, spousal abuse, and escaping abuse are all significant challenges that can impact an individual's mental health and well-being. These challenges can lead to a sense of disconnection and isolation, making it difficult to form meaningful relationships and engage in fulfilling activities.

However, for Christians, turning to their faith can provide a source of comfort and guidance. Spiritual practices such as prayer, Bible reading, and fellowship with other believers can help individuals connect with a higher power and provide a sense of purpose and direction. In particular, prayer has been found to have positive effects on mental health, reducing symptoms of anxiety and depression and improving overall well-being (Amen & Hanks, 2011).

While seeking support from a religious community can be beneficial, it's important to note that it's not a substitute for professional help. Individuals dealing with mental health challenges should seek the help of a trained mental health professional in addition to turning to their faith for guidance and support.

It's also important to recognize that not all individuals may identify as Christian, and therefore may not find comfort in turning to religious practices for guidance. In such cases, it's essential to promote a range of resources and support systems that can help individuals facing these challenges, including therapy, support groups, and other forms of social support.

In summary, while challenges such as apathy, lack of belonging, low self-esteem, discontentment, marriage problems, spousal abuse, and escaping abuse can have a profound impact on an individual's mental health and well-being, turning to religious practices such as prayer, Bible reading, and fellowship with other believers can provide a sense of comfort and guidance for Christians. However, it's important to recognize that this is not a substitute for professional help and that a range of resources and support systems should be promoted to help individuals facing these challenges.

The Story of David and Jane

Meet David and Jane, a Christian married couple who had been struggling with their relationship. David had been in a car wreck and became hooked on opiates due to his intense back pain. He became increasingly angry, controlling, and abusive toward Rebecca, belittling and criticizing her at every opportunity. He didn't understand the influence the drugs had on his emotions. Following the bad example of his father, he began to use physical force to intimidate her and keep her under his control.

Jane tried to talk to David about the abuse, but he refused to listen, and even used his faith as an excuse to justify his actions. He claimed that as the head of the household, he had the right to control his wife and her actions.

Feeling trapped and alone, Jane turned to her pastor for help. Her pastor reminded her that God created marriage to be a partnership based on love, respect, and compassion. He explained that spousal abuse is a serious issue and goes against God's teachings.

With her pastor's help, Jane began to understand that the abuse was not her fault and that she had the right to leave the relationship. The pastor also recommended that David attend counseling and seek guidance from the church. David was hesitant at first but eventually agreed to attend counseling. With the help of a Christian counselor, David began to see the damage that his behavior was causing to their marriage and to his wife's mental health.

Making and IMPACT

Through counseling and prayer, David was able to address his controlling and abusive behavior and learned how to show love and respect towards his wife. He also addressed his drug use and became more involved in the Celebrate Recovery group at church. He began to lean on his faith and church family to guide him in his actions.

Today, David and Jane's relationship has improved, and they are both committed to building a loving and supportive marriage based on Christian values. They understand that marriage problems can arise, but that it is important to seek help and guidance from the church and their faith during difficult times. They also know that spousal abuse is never acceptable and that God calls us to love and cherish our spouses, not to control and abuse them. As is illustrated in the relationship between Christ and his bride, the church: Christ loved his bride so much that he laid down his life for her.

Some Possible Solutions with Coping Skills

Engaging in activities and acquiring knowledge about topics that one is passionate about can have numerous benefits beyond simply providing enjoyment. It can lead to increased motivation, higher self-esteem, and a greater sense of purpose and fulfillment in life. For example, a person who is passionate about history may become motivated to learn more about the subject by reading books, visiting historical sites, or engaging in discussions with others who share their interest. This increased motivation can spill over into other areas of their life, such as their career or personal relationships, leading to greater success and satisfaction.

In addition, learning about something that one is passionate about can lead to a greater sense of self-awareness and understanding. As individuals delve deeper into their interests, they may gain insights into their values, strengths, and weaknesses, which can be applied to other areas of their life. For instance, someone who is passionate about science may learn more about critical thinking, problem-solving, and experimentation, which can be applied to other areas of their life such as their job or personal relationships.

Furthermore, engaging in activities related to one's passion can provide a sense of community and connection with others who share the same interest. This can lead to new friendships, networking opportunities, and a greater sense of belonging. For instance, someone who is passionate about technology may attend workshops or join online communities to connect with others who share their interest, leading to a greater sense of connection and camaraderie.

Overall, learning about something one is passionate about can lead to a greater sense of fulfillment and success in many areas of life. By exploring one's interests and engaging in related activities, individuals can gain motivation, self-awareness, community, and many other benefits that can lead to a more fulfilling and satisfying life.

Skydiving is a recreational activity that involves jumping from an aircraft at high altitude and freefalling before deploying a parachute to slow descent and safely land on the ground. For many people, skydiving is an opportunity to experience the thrill and excitement of flight, pushing the limits of the human body and mind. The experience can be exhilarating and provide an adrenaline rush, as well as a  sense of accomplishment and empowerment. The experience of skydiving can also serve as a way for individuals to confront and overcome their fears, such as the fear of heights or the fear of failure. By facing these fears and taking on a challenge, individuals can develop confidence and resilience, which can positively impact other areas of their life. However, it is important to note that skydiving carries inherent risks, and safety precautions must be taken to ensure a safe and successful jump. Proper training, equipment, and experienced instructors are essential for mitigating these risks and ensuring the safety of participants. Overall, skydiving can provide a unique and exciting adventure, with the potential to push individuals out of their comfort zone and help them overcome fears and limitations.

Creating new relationships is a fundamental aspect of human life that can bring many positive benefits to our well-being. Research suggests that social support is associated with a variety of positive outcomes, including lower levels of stress, reduced risk of developing mental health issues, and increased resilience in the face of adversity.

Joining a church, small Bible study group, volunteer group, or social organization can provide an opportunity to meet new people who share similar interests and values, leading to the formation of new relationships. These relationships can be a source of social support, providing a sense of belonging, empathy, and validation. Additionally, these relationships can foster a sense of camaraderie and shared purpose, encouraging individuals to work together towards a common goal.

Moreover, belonging to a group can provide a sense of identity and purpose, helping individuals feel like they are a part of something larger than themselves. This sense of belonging and identity can be especially important during times of transition or uncertainty, such as moving to a new city or going through a major life change.

However, it is important to note that forming new relationships and joining new groups can also present challenges. For example, individuals may feel anxious or hesitant about meeting new people, especially if they have experienced rejection or social anxiety in the past. Additionally, relationships can be complex and may require time and effort to develop and maintain.

Overall, forming new relationships with like-minded individuals can provide a sense of belonging, support, and camaraderie, and can be an important part of maintaining overall well-being. However, it is important to approach these new relationships with an open mind and to be aware of the challenges that may arise.

Marriage counseling is a type of therapy that is designed to help couples improve their relationship and resolve conflicts. It can be a valuable tool for couples who are experiencing challenges in their marriage, as it provides a safe and supportive environment for couples to work through their problems. The goal of marriage counseling is to help couples improve communication, build stronger emotional bonds, and establish healthier patterns of behavior.

One of the benefits of seeking marriage counseling is that it can provide a neutral third party to help couples work through their issues. A trained counselor can help couples identify the underlying causes of their problems and develop strategies to overcome them. This can include teaching couples communication skills, conflict resolution techniques, and ways to deepen their emotional connection.

Making and IMPACT

Many pastors offer marriage counseling services as part of their ministry. Pastoral counseling can be particularly appealing to religious couples, as it allows them to integrate their faith into the counseling process. Pastoral counselors may also be better equipped to address spiritual and religious issues that may be impacting the couple's relationship.

Marriage counseling is not a one-size-fits-all solution. The success of counseling depends on the willingness of both partners to actively participate in the process and work towards a resolution. Additionally, some couples may require more intensive therapy, such as individual counseling or group therapy, in order to address their specific needs.

Despite the challenges, marriage counseling can be a valuable tool for couples who are committed to improving their relationship. By seeking help from a trained counselor, couples can gain the skills and insights they need to overcome challenges and build a stronger, more fulfilling relationship.

Engaging in a new hobby is not only a great way to channel creativity, but also to stimulate the brain and cultivate a sense of personal fulfillment. Pursuing new hobbies provides an opportunity to learn and develop new skills, which can enhance cognitive function and build self-esteem. The act of creating something can be a highly rewarding experience, providing a sense of accomplishment that can boost confidence and improve overall well-being.

Moreover, participating in a new hobby can provide a much-needed break from the stresses of daily life. By redirecting attention to an enjoyable and absorbing activity, individuals can recharge their mental and emotional batteries, and reduce the negative effects of stress on the mind and body.

Additionally, the social benefits of new hobbies should not be overlooked. Engaging in a new activity can provide an opportunity to connect with like-minded individuals and form new friendships. This can be especially important for those who may be looking for ways to expand their social circles or are seeking to meet others who share similar interests.

For example, a person who takes up painting may join a local art club, which provides an opportunity to interact with others who share the same passion. This can help individuals develop a sense of community and belonging, which is essential for overall mental health and well-being.

Taking up a new hobby can offer a range of benefits, including providing an outlet for creativity, reducing stress, and building new social connections.

Making and IMPACT

As a result, it can be a valuable addition to an individual's self-care routine, and a way to enhance overall quality of life.

Participating in community service can have numerous positive effects on both individuals and society as a whole. Volunteering in a local church or school drug abuse program can be a particularly impactful way to give back and make a difference. By working with young people and providing them with support and resources to prevent drug abuse and addiction, volunteers can help to build stronger, healthier communities.

Volunteering in a drug abuse program can also be a valuable experience for the volunteer themselves. Research has shown that volunteering can have a positive impact on mental health and well-being, reducing stress and providing a sense of purpose and fulfillment. Additionally, volunteering can help to build social connections and a sense of belonging, further contributing to overall well-being.

Working in a drug abuse program can also provide individuals with the opportunity to learn more about addiction and its effects on individuals and society. This knowledge can be valuable in many fields, including healthcare, social work, and public policy. By contributing to a drug abuse program, volunteers can gain practical experience and develop skills that can be useful in a wide range of settings.

Overall, volunteering in a local church or school drug abuse program can be a meaningful and fulfilling way to give back to the community and make a positive impact on the lives of others. It can also provide volunteers with valuable experiences and knowledge that can benefit them personally and professionally.

Physical activity has been shown to have numerous benefits for both physical and mental health. Engaging in activities such as walking, running, or participating in marathons can improve cardiovascular health, build muscle, and increase endurance. Exercise has also been shown to improve mood, reduce stress and anxiety, and enhance overall mental well-being.

Physical activity stimulates the release of endorphins, neurotransmitters that produce feelings of pleasure and reduce pain. This natural high can help to reduce stress and improve mood, making exercise a powerful tool for maintaining mental health. In addition, regular exercise can improve self-esteem and body image, which can have positive effects on mental health and overall well-being.

The benefits of physical activity are not just limited to physical and mental health. Engaging in regular exercise can also provide opportunities for social connection and community involvement. For example, participating in a running club or fitness class can offer the chance to meet like-minded individuals and form new friendships.

It's important to note that physical activity should be approached in a safe and sustainable manner. Overexertion or improper technique can lead to injury or other negative consequences. Additionally, it's important to engage in physical activity that is appropriate for one's current level of fitness and health.

Physical activity can provide numerous benefits for both physical and mental health. Regular exercise can improve mood, reduce stress, and enhance overall well-being, while also providing opportunities for social connection and community involvement. Approach physical activity in a safe and sustainable manner to maximize its benefits.

For those who enjoy the outdoors, hunting and fishing can provide opportunities for adventure, relaxation, and connection with nature. These activities can also provide a sense of accomplishment and a break from the demands of daily life.

Hiking, camping, and other outdoor adventures provide an opportunity to explore nature and its natural beauty, which can have a positive impact on an individual's physical and mental health. Outdoor activities, particularly those that involve physical activity, have been shown to improve physical fitness, reduce stress levels, and increase feelings of well-being.

The search for elusive creatures like Bigfoot may add an extra element of excitement to these activities for some people. While some unbelievers say there is no scientific evidence to support the existence of Bigfoot, the search for this and other cryptids (animals that cryptozoologists believe may exist somewhere in the wild, but are not recognized by science) can still be a fun and engaging experience for many. Your kids will love looking for Bigfoot, and you'll find a new way to connect with your family. By the way, the excitement of the unknown can stimulate the release of dopamine in the brain, which is associated with feelings of pleasure and reward.

In addition to the potential for pleasure and excitement, outdoor activities can also offer an opportunity for personal growth and discovery. So go camping. Through exploration and adventure, individuals may gain new perspectives and insights about themselves and the world around them. This can lead to increased confidence, self-awareness, and personal fulfillment.

Outdoor activities also come with risks and require proper preparation and safety precautions. Study outdoor survival before you go. Individuals engaging in these activities should be aware of potential hazards and should take the necessary steps to ensure their safety and the safety of others.

Outdoor activities such as hiking, camping, and exploring nature can provide numerous physical, mental, and emotional benefits. While the search for Bigfoot or other cryptids may add an element of excitement to these activities, it is the exploration and discovery of nature that truly offers the most profound and rewarding experiences.

While coping mechanisms can be valuable in managing difficult situations, there are times when they may not be appropriate or effective. For instance, in cases of physical abuse, relying solely on coping skills is not a sufficient solution. In such situations, it may be necessary to remove oneself from the situation entirely for the sake of safety and well-being. It is important to recognize that individuals have agency over their own lives and are responsible for making decisions that are in their best interest. The decision to use coping mechanisms or to remove oneself from a situation should be a deliberate and informed one. In some cases, both approaches may be necessary, such as in situations where it may not be immediately possible to leave but coping mechanisms can help in the short-term. Ultimately, the most effective approach will depend on the specific circumstances of the situation and the individual's personal preferences and needs.

Making and IMPACT

Drug Use vs. Coping Skills

While drugs may provide immediate relief, they come with a host of negative consequences that can severely impact an individual's long-term well-being. In contrast, healthy coping mechanisms, such as exercise, meditation, or therapy, may not provide the same immediate effects but can have numerous benefits over the long term. Healthy coping mechanisms have been shown to reduce stress, improve mood, and enhance overall well-being.

Additionally, while coping mechanisms such as engaging in hobbies or pursuing new experiences can provide a temporary escape, it is important to recognize when these activities begin to have negative consequences. If engaging in a hobby begins to interfere with daily life and relationships, it may be time to reevaluate its role as a coping mechanism.

Ultimately, the choice between drugs and healthy coping mechanisms comes down to choosing short-term relief versus long-term well-being. While it may be tempting to seek immediate relief through drugs, the negative consequences can be severe and long-lasting. Choosing healthy coping mechanisms may require more effort and time, but they offer a sustainable and healthy way to manage stress and emotions, leading to a more fulfilling and stable life.

Your Default Coping Skill

The concept of default behaviors is an important one, as it can shed light on how individuals develop coping mechanisms and habits that can either help or harm them. In the case of drug addiction, the release of "happy chemicals" such as endorphins, serotonin, and dopamine can create a powerful association between drug use and pleasure. Over time, this can lead to the development of default coping skills that involve the use of drugs to manage stress, anxiety, and other negative emotions.

Understanding the development of default coping skills is crucial to addressing addiction and promoting healthier behaviors. By recognizing the underlying factors that contribute to the development of default behaviors, such as past experiences or cultural influences, individuals can begin to identify healthier coping mechanisms that can replace drug use. For example, a person who grew up playing baseball as a way to cope with anger may benefit from exploring other forms of physical activity, such as running or swimming.

Making and IMPACT

Breaking away from default coping skills can be challenging and may require support from a therapist or other mental health professional. In some cases, medication may be necessary to help manage withdrawal symptoms or other medical complications associated with drug addiction.

The concept of default coping skills sheds light on the allure of drug use as a quick solution to dealing with life's problems. Our brains are wired to seek out the most efficient and effective way of dealing with stress and negative emotions. In the short term, drugs may provide the highest level of relief, as they can artificially stimulate the release of "happy chemicals" in the brain. This creates a challenge for natural

coping mechanisms, like playing baseball or other hobbies, to compete with the intensity of drug use. However, it is crucial to recognize that relying on drugs can lead to severe consequences, including addiction, health problems, and legal issues, while natural coping mechanisms are generally safe and sustainable.

While natural coping mechanisms may not provide the same intensity of relief as drugs, they can still be effective in managing stress and negative emotions, especially when practiced regularly. Over time, natural coping mechanisms can help to rewire the brain and establish healthier default coping skills.

In the journey towards recovery, individuals must accept that they will no longer have the same intense experience with drugs, but in return, they can avoid the negative consequences that come with drug use. By developing healthier default coping skills, individuals can cultivate a greater sense of control and stability in their lives, and experience the long-term benefits of sustained emotional well-being.

Communication Leads to Success

Effective communication is a crucial aspect of the recovery process, and its importance cannot be overstated. However, many individuals may struggle with effective communication due to a lack of necessary skills and training. Although some may have taken public speaking courses during their academic years, they may not have developed personal communication skills through interactions with family and friends.

The Bible offers many directives about communication, such as "Let no corrupting talk come out of your mouths, but only such as is good for building up, as fits the occasion, that it may give grace to those who hear." (Eph. 4:29) And "Let your speech always be gracious, seasoned with salt, so that you may know how you ought to answer each person." (Col. 4:6).

The most important aspect of communication in the Bible is "…the Word became flesh and dwelt among us" (John 1:14). God knew the only way to communicate his powerful love to the world was to become flesh, to join us in the struggle, to completely identify with us. Improving our ability to communicate can help everyone in the struggle against substance abuse. Therefore, it is essential to consider the means to effective communication.

By seeking guidance from the Bible and practicing communication skills, a Christian can improve their ability to communicate and build meaningful relationships. This can involve learning to listen actively, expressing oneself clearly and honestly, and practicing compassion and empathy. Through effective communication, individuals in recovery can build support networks, receive guidance and encouragement, and cultivate a sense of purpose and meaning.

Aspects of Effective Communication

In counseling and therapy, effective communication is of utmost importance. Both the counselor and the client must understand its significance and possess the necessary skills to effectively transmit and receive information. This is particularly crucial in group therapy sessions, as well as in individual and family therapy. For clients to achieve and maintain long-term recovery, they must be able to express their feelings and communicate effectively with their loved ones, colleagues, and friends.

Effective communication is a two-way process, and both the counselor and client must have a clear understanding of how to navigate it successfully. In order to avoid any potential hindrances to recovery, it is important that both parties have a clear understanding of the communication process and the skills necessary to effectively communicate with one another.

Effective communication is a critical aspect of recovery from SUD. It involves the process of sending and receiving messages in a way that ensures that the message is understood as intended. Miscommunication can lead to a range of negative outcomes, including strained relationships, damaged friendships, failed marriages, and unproductive or closed businesses. To ensure successful communication, it is important to identify and remove any barriers to effective communication at every stage of the process.

The stages of effective communication include the source of the message, the nature of the message, the encoding process, the method of transmission, the decoding process, the destination of the message, and the feedback process between the transmitter and receiver. Each of these stages plays a crucial role in ensuring successful communication, and any barriers present at any of these stages can lead to misunderstandings and miscommunication.

Therefore, pay attention to the various stages of communication and to remove any barriers that may exist. This can be achieved by being clear, concise, and direct in the message, using appropriate language and tone, and ensuring that the message is transmitted through the most effective method. Additionally, it is important to provide feedback and to listen actively to the receiver to ensure that the message has been understood correctly.

Making and IMPACT

The role of communication (with or without the impact of emotional baggage) is a critical aspect of recovery from SUD, and it plays a key role in maintaining healthy relationships, resolving conflicts, and promoting personal and professional growth.

The Source or Transmitter

Making a positive first impression when communicating is crucial, as it can greatly influence the receiver's willingness to receive the message. The transmitter can demonstrate their openness and friendliness by offering a handshake, smiling, and presenting themselves well with appropriate grooming and attire. The perceived value of the message is closely linked to the perceived value of the transmitter, and by presenting themselves professionally and respectfully, the transmitter can increase the value of the message.

The attitudes of the transmitter and receiver can have a significant impact on the outcome of the communication. A positive attitude from the transmitter can encourage a positive attitude from the receiver, while a negative attitude can have the opposite effect. To be effective in communication, the transmitter must exhibit assertiveness, but it is important to avoid becoming aggressive, as this can obstruct the message. To be successful, the transmitter must be adaptable and adjust their message encoding to match the response or feedback from the receiver.

Effective communication also requires the ability to organize and present the message in a clear and concise manner. By making sure the message is simple, well-organized, and easy to understand, the receiver is more likely to perceive the message as valuable and be open to receiving it. It is important to be patient and calmly restate the message in simple terms, without a condescending attitude, to help the receiver understand and process the information.

Nature of the Message

In communication, it is important to ensure that the message being conveyed is relevant to the intended audience. Different groups of people have different needs and perspectives, and it is important to tailor the message accordingly. For example, it would not be appropriate to present the same drug education material to hardened criminals as to adolescents experimenting with drugs for the first time.

To effectively communicate, the transmitter must have a comprehensive understanding of the message and the audience it is intended for. It is also essential to verify the accuracy of the information included in the message, as misinformation can erode trust between the transmitter and receiver. For instance, if a transmitter makes a false statement, such as "there are more males with HIV in this city than any other city in the world," and the receiver is aware that this is not accurate, they may disregard the rest of the message and question the transmitter's credibility.

To engage the receiver and ensure understanding, it is crucial to emphasize the importance of the message and provide motivation for the receiver to incorporate it into their life. The message should be presented in a logical and coherent manner, and be factually accurate, culturally relevant, personally valuable, and motivational for the receiver.

The Encoding Process

It is important to tailor the message to the specific audience it is being delivered to. Different drug education materials would be presented to hardened criminals than to adolescents experimenting with drugs for the first time, for example. To effectively communicate, the transmitter must have a deep understanding of the message and the audience it is being presented to.

Moreover, it is crucial to verify the accuracy of the information included in the message to maintain the receiver's trust in the transmitter. Misinformation in the message can cause the receiver to disengage and ignore the rest of the message.

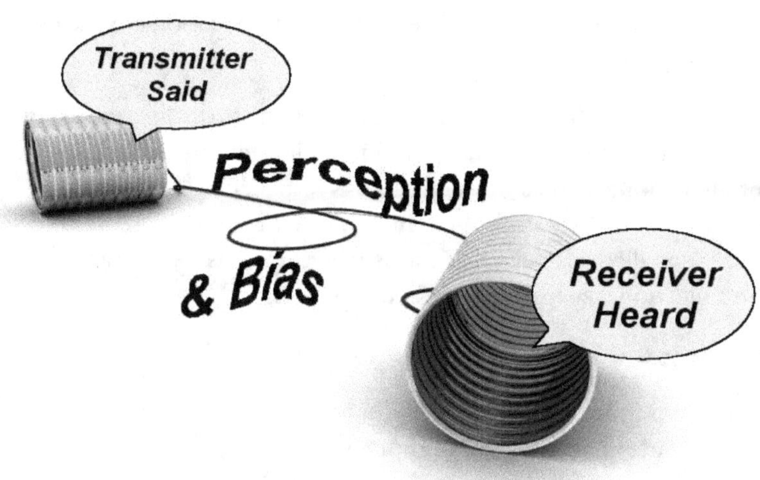

To make the message appealing and engaging to the receiver, it is essential to present it in an interesting and relatable manner. This can be achieved by using humor, heart-warming thoughts, or other emotions that resonate with the receiver, which can add value to the message and make it more appealing.

In addition to understanding the message and the audience, it is important to adjust the encoding of the message to match the receiver's willingness and ability to understand, taking into account their culture, environment, and relationships. This will ensure that the message is received willingly and graciously.

The Method of Communication

Effective communication involves not only the content of the message, but also the method by which it is conveyed. To ensure the successful transmission of the message, it is important to use a method of communication that is familiar and well-versed in. This not only allows the audience to receive the message, but it also enhances the perceived value of the message through the transmitter's expertise in delivery.

There are various methods of communication that can be employed, including face-to-face interactions, phone calls, text messages, emails, and video chats. Face-to-face interactions are particularly effective for personal communication, as they allow for the exchange of non-verbal cues, such as body language, which can provide a deeper understanding between the transmitter and receiver.

However, it is important to note that in certain situations, such as when individuals may be hiding information, the limitations of text-based communication, such as the lack of non-verbal cues, may make it a less effective method. In cases where individuals may feel pressure to disengage from potentially harmful situations, such as drug use, text-based communication may prove to be a useful tool.

Decoding the Message

Effective communication requires not only the efforts of the transmitter to encode the message in a clear and precise manner, but also the efforts of the receiver to actively listen, read, or interpret the message in a way that accurately captures its intended meaning. The receiver plays a crucial role in the communication process by engaging actively in the decoding process and using their knowledge, skills, and experience to interpret the message correctly.

To ensure that the message is received and understood as intended, the transmitter must take into account the necessary prerequisites of the receiver, such as relevant background information, technical knowledge, education, or cultural understanding. By recognizing the vital role of the receiver in the communication process, the transmitter can take steps to ensure that the receiver has the necessary tools and understanding to properly decode the message.

Effective communication requires a collaborative effort between the transmitter and receiver, with each playing a critical role in the process. The transmitter must encode the message in a clear and precise manner, while the receiver must actively listen, read, or interpret the message, using their knowledge, skills, and experience to ensure that the message is accurately understood. By recognizing the importance of both the transmitter and the receiver in the communication process, the message can be effectively conveyed and understood.

Know the Receiver

When delivering a message, it is important to be mindful of the receiver's level of education, experience, and limitations. For example, the approach taken when discussing the topic of drug use with a hardened criminal who has been incarcerated for 20 years would be vastly different from that of a teenager who may be experimenting with drugs for the first time. This is because the receiver's pre-existing knowledge and understanding of the topic can affect their ability to comprehend the message being presented.

Additionally, it is crucial for the transmitter to take into account the cultural knowledge, biases, and prejudices of the receiver. For instance, individuals who have struggled with drug addiction may be distrustful of counselors who have never personally experienced drug use. In this scenario, it is essential for the transmitter to express empathy and true understanding, and to use positive feedback as a guide to effectively communicate the message of recovery.

Effective communication requires an understanding of the receiver's background, experiences, and cultural knowledge. By taking these factors into consideration, the transmitter can tailor the message to ensure that it is accurately understood and received. In doing so, the transmitter can increase the effectiveness of the message and promote a positive outcome for the receiver.

Provide Feedback

Effective communication requires a keen focus on the audience, both as individuals and as a collective group. By carefully observing the audience, the transmitter can gain valuable insights into how the message is being received through verbal and non-verbal feedback.

One important aspect of this feedback is the receiver's body language, which can provide valuable information about their level of understanding and engagement with the message. By paying attention to nonverbal cues such as facial expressions, posture, and gestures, the transmitter can gain a deeper understanding of how the message is being received and make adjustments to the encoding and transmission of the message as necessary to ensure it is understood clearly. For example, if the receiver appears confused or disengaged, the transmitter may need to rephrase or re-explain the message in a different way.

Furthermore, paying close attention to verbal feedback, such as questions or comments, can also assist in refining the message to best meet the needs of the receiver. By actively engaging with the audience and taking their feedback into consideration, the transmitter can improve the effectiveness of the communication and ensure that the message is accurately understood and received. Effective communication requires a two-way dialogue between the transmitter and receiver, with both parties playing a critical role in the process.

Context of the Message

An attentive transmitter takes into account the context in which the message is being delivered. This includes the specific situation and environment in which the message is presented, as well as the culture of the audience, whether it be in a state, country, corporation, or other setting.

Ignoring or not properly considering the context in which the message is being delivered can greatly hinder its success. For example, when communicating with a group of drug users in a prison setting, a realistic, straightforward, and "tough" approach, using appropriate prison slang, would be necessary. On the other hand, when addressing a group of corporate executives, a sophisticated and polished message with proper grammar and etiquette would be expected.

Therefore, it is crucial for the transmitter to have a comprehensive understanding of the context in which the message is being delivered, in order to effectively tailor the message to meet the needs of the receiver and maximize its reception and comprehension. Effective communication requires not only the transmission of a clear and concise message, but also a thorough understanding of the audience and the context in which the message is being delivered.

The 7 C's of Communication

The seven C's of effective communication serve as a comprehensive framework for both counselors and clients to effectively communicate and receive information. These seven elements, namely Clarity, Conciseness, Completeness, Consideration, Concreteness, Correctness, and Courteousness, are designed to assist individuals in conveying their message in a clear, concise, and complete manner. By incorporating these elements, the message will be more likely to be understood and received in the manner intended, thereby promoting effective communication and mutual understanding. It is important to remember that effective communication is a two-way process and requires active engagement from both parties to ensure that the intended message is received and understood correctly.

Clarity is a critical aspect of effective communication as it lays the foundation for a clear understanding of the purpose and intent behind a message. A message that is clear and concise is more likely to be received and understood correctly, as it eliminates any potential for confusion or misinterpretation. In order to achieve clarity in communication, it is essential to simplify the message and present it in a straightforward and easy-to-understand manner. The use of simple and direct language, along with minimizing the amount of information presented, can help prevent assumptions and misunderstandings.

Moreover, clarity helps to ensure that the message is aligned with the intended purpose, and that both the sender and the receiver have a common understanding of what is being conveyed. This is especially important in professional or formal settings where misunderstandings can have serious consequences. Therefore, it is imperative that individuals take the time to carefully craft their messages with clarity in mind, to ensure that they are effectively communicating their intended message and promoting clear understanding.

Conciseness plays a vital role in effective communication by making sure that the message is short, simple, and direct. This helps to keep the audience engaged and focused, as well as ensuring that the intended message is received and understood. By eliminating unnecessary sentences, redundant information, and rambling thoughts, the message can be kept concise and to the point, thereby avoiding confusion or misinterpretation.

In today's fast-paced society, people are often bombarded with an overwhelming amount of information and it is important to be able to convey a message that is brief and easy to understand. Concise messages are more likely to be remembered and acted upon, as they do not overload the audience with information. Additionally, conciseness helps to build credibility and trust, as it demonstrates that the speaker has taken the time to carefully consider their message and present it in a clear and direct manner.

Strive for conciseness in their communication, to ensure that their message is received and understood effectively. Whether it is in professional or personal settings, a concise message is more likely to grab the audience's attention and leave a lasting impression.

Concreteness is a crucial aspect of effective communication as it helps to create a clear and vivid picture of the topic being discussed. It is important to provide specific and relevant details that help to make the message more interesting and memorable. By using descriptive and concrete language, individuals are able to bring the message to life and make it more relatable to the audience.

Concreteness is also important in helping to prevent misunderstandings and confusion, as it provides the audience with a clear understanding of the topic being discussed. For example, instead of saying "some substance use has really increased," it would be more concrete to say "fentanyl use has increased by 28% in this neighborhood compared to last year." This type of concrete  information is more likely to be remembered and acted upon, as it provides a clear and specific picture of the situation.

In addition, concreteness can also help to make the message more engaging and dynamic. By using colorful and vivid descriptions, individuals can bring their message to life and make it more interesting and memorable. This can help to keep the audience engaged and focused, and can also help to build credibility and trust, as it demonstrates that the speaker has taken the time to carefully consider their message and present it in a concrete and vivid manner.

Therefore, it is important to strive for concreteness in communication, as it helps to create a clear and vivid picture of the topic being discussed, while also helping to prevent misunderstandings and confusion. By using concrete and descriptive language, individuals can effectively communicate their message and promote a better understanding of the topic at hand.

Correctness is a critical aspect of effective communication, as it ensures that the facts presented are accurate and the language used is clear and error-free. In order to promote clear and effective communication, it is essential to take the time to proofread the message and check for any errors or inaccuracies. This includes checking for correct grammar, spelling, and punctuation, as well as ensuring that the information presented is accurate and up-to-date.

Inaccurate information or errors in grammar or spelling can detract from the credibility of the message and lead to misunderstandings or confusion. In professional settings, it is especially important to ensure that the message is free from errors, as incorrect information can have serious consequences. Furthermore, a message that is well-written and error-free is more likely to be taken seriously and considered by the audience.

While computer spell-checkers can be a useful tool in catching spelling errors, it is important to remember that they are not perfect and may not catch every mistake. Therefore, it is essential to take the time to carefully proofread the message and double-check for any errors or inaccuracies. This can help to ensure that the message is clear and effective, and that the intended message is received and understood correctly.

Correctness is a vital aspect of effective communication and must be considered in order to promote clear and accurate communication. By taking the time to proofread the message and ensure that the facts presented are accurate, individuals can help to build credibility and promote clear and effective communication.

Coherency is an essential aspect of effective communication, as it ensures that the message is logical, connected, and relevant to the main topic. A message that is coherent and well-organized is more likely to be received and understood correctly, as it helps to keep the audience focused and engaged.

Coherency involves presenting information in a logical and structured manner, with clear connections between the different parts of the message. This helps to ensure that the message is easy to follow and understand, and that the audience is able to see the relevance of the information presented. In order to maintain coherency, it is important to have a clear understanding of the main topic and to stay focused on that topic throughout the message.

Writing down the spoken message in advance can also be a helpful tool in promoting coherency. This allows individuals to organize their thoughts and structure the message in a logical and coherent manner. It also provides an opportunity to review and edit the message, making any necessary adjustments to ensure that the message is clear, concise, and on track.

Coherency is a critical aspect of effective communication and plays an important role in ensuring that the message is received and understood correctly. By maintaining a clear and logical structure, and by staying focused on the main topic, individuals can help to promote coherency and ensure that their message is clear and effective.

Completeness is a crucial aspect of effective communication, as it ensures that the audience receives all the necessary information in order to fully understand the message. A message that is complete and comprehensive is more likely to be received and understood correctly, as it provides the audience with all the information they need to know.

Completeness involves providing all relevant details, such as time, date, place, and names. This information helps to provide context and clarity, and allows the audience to understand the message in its entirety. For example, when communicating about a meeting, it is important to provide the time, date, and location, as well as any other relevant information, such as the purpose of the meeting or the expected outcomes.

In order to ensure completeness in communication, it is important to carefully consider the audience and what information they need to know. This may involve taking the time to gather all relevant details and presenting them in a clear and organized manner. By providing complete and comprehensive information, individuals can help to build credibility and promote clear and effective communication.

Completeness is a critical aspect of effective communication and plays an important role in ensuring that the audience receives all the necessary information. By providing complete and relevant information, individuals can help to promote clear and effective communication, and ensure that their message is received and understood correctly.

Courteousness is a key component of effective communication, as it ensures that the message is delivered in a friendly, open, and honest manner. This approach is particularly important when communicating with individuals who use drugs, as it can help to build trust and respect, which are essential for effective communication.

Being courteous in communication involves using language and tone that is respectful and non-judgmental. This can help to create a safe and supportive environment, where individuals feel comfortable sharing their thoughts and feelings. By using a courteous approach, individuals can help to build rapport and establish a positive relationship, which can be critical in promoting effective communication.

In addition, courteousness can also help to promote understanding and empathy, as it demonstrates a genuine interest in the well-being and needs of the other person. This approach can help to create a positive and supportive environment, where individuals feel comfortable discussing sensitive and personal topics.

Therefore, express courteousness in communication, particularly when working with individuals who use drugs. Working with substance abusers in a correctional facility, gaining respect with courteousness is one of the most important means of ensuring that client's willing to listen. By using a friendly, open, and honest approach, individuals can help to build trust and respect, and promote clear and effective communication. This can be critical in promoting a positive and supportive environment, where individuals feel comfortable and heard.

Poor Communication Example

In the scenario described, the father's approach to expressing his thoughts and opinions regarding the dinner dish was not effective, leading to a miscommunication between him and the mother. When the father mentioned that the previous Taco Soup was bland and suggested adding more seasoning, the mother may have interpreted this as a criticism of her cooking, rather than a suggestion for improvement.

To improve the flow of communication in this scenario, the father could have taken a more constructive and supportive approach. By expressing that he was looking forward to trying the new version of the dish, and by phrasing his suggestion in a positive and supportive manner, the father could have helped to avoid any misunderstandings or hurt feelings.

In a scenario of effective communication, the father would have taken the time to express his thoughts and opinions in a clear and supportive manner. By expressing his appreciation for the mother's cooking, and by asking for her feedback and showing interest in her opinion, the father could have helped to promote a positive and productive conversation, where both individuals feel heard and understood.

It is important to remember that communication is a two-way process, and both parties play a role in ensuring that the message is received and understood correctly. By taking the time to express thoughts and opinions in a clear and supportive manner, and by actively listening and seeking feedback from the other party, individuals can help to promote effective communication and build strong and positive relationships.

Aspects of Effective Communication: Listening

Effective communication is a vital component in professional settings, and active listening plays a key role in this process. As a presenter, it is important to monitor the audience's engagement and attention, and to take steps to maintain their interest. One way to assess this is by observing the group's body language and considering the average attention span, which is typically around 20 minutes. To keep the audience engaged, it is recommended to schedule regular breaks and to plan the presentation in a manner that keeps the audience interested.

It is also important to be aware of defensive listening, where some individuals may be resistant to change or may challenge the material being presented. To address this, it is important to acknowledge any core issues that may be preventing the audience from being open to the information, and to find ways to address these concerns. Giving the audience opportunities to restate the information can also help to ensure that the information is being understood and retained.

In addition, it is important to recognize that not all information presented may be entirely accurate. As a presenter, it is recommended to familiarize oneself with the material beforehand, and to add a personal perspective to make the presentation more engaging. By acknowledging any gaps in the information and providing a personal perspective, the presenter can help to promote a more effective and engaging presentation.

Effective communication can also have a profound impact on individuals and families struggling with substance abuse. Families often suffer the most from ineffective communication skills. Often families try to ignore the problem hoping it will fix itself, but that is rarely the case. Drug use that is never confronted or treated will usually progress until it ends in either prison or death.

Miscommunication among individuals with families, friends, and others can lead to frustration and relapse, but effective communication can help to promote understanding and positive change. Former substance users can become powerful motivational speakers by sharing their experiences and insights with others. Through effective communication, it is possible to positively impact many others and potentially even save lives.

The Family Dynamics of SUD

Impact of SUD on Family Life

The impact of Substance Use Disorder (SUD) on family life can be devastating. Substance abuse can lead to changes in behavior that can cause conflict and tension within the family. The individual struggling with substance use may become unpredictable, irritable, or violent, causing fear and anxiety for other family members.

Children, in particular, can be deeply affected by a parent or caregiver's substance abuse. Neglect or abuse can result in emotional, behavioral, and developmental problems that can last a lifetime. Children may experience trauma, depression, anxiety, and low self-esteem, and may be more likely to engage in substance abuse themselves in the future.

In addition to the emotional toll, SUD can also put a financial strain on families. The cost of substance abuse treatment, lost wages due to missed work, and legal fees can add up quickly and put a significant financial burden on families.

Families may also feel a sense of shame or embarrassment about their loved one's substance abuse, leading to a breakdown in communication and social isolation. Family members may withdraw from friends and activities, leading to feelings of loneliness and isolation.

Despite these challenges, families can play an important role in the recovery process. Family support and involvement in treatment can help the individual struggling with SUD to build a strong support network, increase their chances of success in recovery, and promote healing within the family.

With the right resources and support, families can overcome the challenges of SUD and work towards a brighter future together.

Understanding the Family System

Understanding the dynamics of a family system is crucial when it comes to addressing SUD. Substance abuse can have far-reaching impacts on the entire family system, affecting relationships, communication, and overall functioning.

Family systems theory posits that the family is a complex system in which each member influences and is influenced by the other members. This dynamic can lead to patterns of behavior that enable or perpetuate SUD. For example, a family member may cover for the individual struggling with substance abuse, enabling their substance use to continue. In return, the individual with SUD may feel a sense of loyalty to the family member, further perpetuating the cycle of abuse.

Substance abuse can also disrupt the balance of power within a family system, leading to a breakdown in communication and increased conflict. Family members may take on different roles, such as the enabler, the rescuer, or the scapegoat, which can further exacerbate the problem.

However, it is important to note that family dynamics can also be a source of strength and support in recovery. Families can work together to create a supportive environment that promotes healthy behavior and helps the individual struggling with SUD to maintain sobriety.

The first step in understanding the dynamics of a family system is to recognize the role that each family member plays in the SUD. By recognizing the impact that substance abuse has on the entire family system, families can work together, with the guidance of a professional therapist, to promote healing and support the individual in their journey towards recovery.

The Role of Family in SUD

The role of family in SUD is complex and multifaceted. Family members can play a significant role in both the development and treatment of SUD. Understanding the impact that substance abuse has on the family system is crucial in addressing and overcoming the problem.

Family members can have a profound impact on an individual's substance use, both positively and negatively. For example, a supportive and understanding family can provide a strong foundation for recovery and promote healthy behavior. On the other hand, a lack of support or enabling behavior can perpetuate substance abuse and hinder progress in recovery.

The family can also play a critical role in the treatment of SUD. Family members can support the individual in their journey towards recovery by participating in therapy, attending support groups, and helping to create a sober environment. Family therapy can be particularly beneficial in addressing the underlying issues that contribute to substance abuse and promoting healthy family dynamics.

The Story of Michael

Meet Michael, an alcoholic and drug user who had been struggling with addiction for years. He had lost his job, his friends, and his family due to his drug use, and he felt hopeless and alone. He felt like no one cared, and at this point in life, he didn't even care about himself.

One day, when Michael felt like ending it all, a missionary came to visit Michael in the mission where he was staying the night. The missionary noticed Michael was crying and explained that he was there to offer support and to share his faith with him. At first, Michael was hesitant, thinking the missionary was just a "do-gooder." But the missionary's kind and non-judgmental approach made him feel comfortable. They talked about Michael's addiction and the reasons why he had turned to drugs, the purpose of life, and reasons for living, including restoring his relationship with his family and God.

The missionary shared stories from the Bible that emphasized the importance of family and the role that family plays in supporting one another. He explained that family members could play a crucial role in Michael's journey towards recovery.

With the missionary's help, Michael decided to reach out to his family and seek their support. They were happily responsive, and he attended family therapy with his parents and wife, where they worked together to address the underlying issues that contributed to Michael's substance abuse and promote healthy family dynamics.

Through therapy and support from his family, Michael was able to make positive changes in his life. He learned how to manage his cravings and resist the urge to use drugs, and he also developed new coping skills to deal with stress and other triggers.

The missionary never saw Michael again, but Michael never forgot his influence, guidance, and support throughout his journey towards recovery. With the help of his family and faith, Michael was able to overcome his addiction and rebuild his life.

Today, Michael is maintaining sobriety, has reconnected with his family, and has started sharing with others the hope he found in Christ. He is grateful for the support of the unknown missionary and the guidance of his faith, which helped him find the strength and motivation to overcome his addiction. He knows that he could not have done it alone and is grateful for the love and support of his family.

Importance of Self-Care

However, it is important to recognize that family members may also need support and treatment for their own emotional and mental health. SUD can take a toll on the well-being of family members, leading to feelings of anger, guilt, and shame. Family members may benefit from their own therapy, support groups, or educational resources to help them cope with the effects of substance abuse.

In some cases, family members may also have their own struggles with substance abuse or mental health issues. This can complicate the situation and require a more comprehensive approach to treatment that addresses the needs of the entire family system.

Family Responses to SUD

Family responses to SUD can vary widely, but they often include a mix of emotions such as anger, confusion, guilt, and frustration. The impact of substance abuse on the family system can be significant, leading to strained relationships and a breakdown in communication. Understanding these responses and knowing how to effectively support family members is essential in addressing and overcoming the problem of SUD.

One common response is denial. Family members may be in denial about the extent of the problem or may minimize the effects of substance abuse. This can lead to a lack of action and prevent the individual from seeking help. Family members may also enable the individual's substance abuse by enabling their behavior or ignoring the problem.

Another common response is anger and frustration. Substance abuse can create a lot of conflict within families, leading to feelings of anger and frustration. Family members may feel as though they are not being heard or may feel resentful about the impact of substance abuse on their lives. In some cases, family members may also direct their anger towards the individual struggling with substance abuse, which can further strain relationships.

Guilt is another common response. Family members may feel guilty about their role in the problem or may feel responsible for the individual's substance abuse. This guilt can lead to a sense of hopelessness and prevent family members from seeking help.

Fear is another common response. Family members may be afraid of the individual's behavior and may feel as though they are in danger. They may also be afraid of losing the individual to substance abuse or to the criminal justice system.

Confusion and uncertainty are also common responses to SUD. Family members may not understand the nature of the problem or may be unsure of how to help. They may also feel overwhelmed by the situation and may not know where to turn for support.

Despite these challenges, families can play a critical role in supporting the individual and helping them to overcome SUD. With the right resources and support, families can help to create a supportive environment and promote healthy behavior. Family members can also participate in therapy, attend support groups, and seek education and resources to better understand the problem and how to support their loved one.

Family responses to SUD can be complex and challenging. Understanding these responses and knowing how to effectively support family members is essential in addressing and overcoming the problem. With the right resources and support, families can play an important role in supporting the individual and promoting recovery.

Understanding Family Interventions

Family Therapy for SUD

Family therapy for SUD is a type of therapeutic intervention that involves the entire family system in the treatment process. The goal of family therapy is to help families understand the dynamics that contribute to SUD and to support the individual in their recovery. This type of therapy is based on the idea that substance abuse is not just a problem for the individual but also affects the entire family system.

Family therapy is a collaborative and proactive approach that aims to help families heal and rebuild their relationships. The therapist works with the entire family to identify the underlying causes of the substance abuse and to develop a plan for recovery. Family therapy helps families to understand the role they play in the individual's substance abuse and how they can support them in their recovery.

One of the key components of family therapy is education. The therapist provides the family with information about SUD and the effects it can have on the individual and the family. This helps families to understand the problem and to see that it is not just the individual's problem but a problem that affects the entire family.

Another important component of family therapy is communication skills training. The therapist works with the family to improve communication and to promote a more positive and supportive environment. This can involve teaching family members how to listen and communicate effectively, how to express their feelings and concerns, and how to provide support to the individual in their recovery.

Family therapy also helps families to address any conflicts or issues that may have arisen as a result of the substance abuse. The therapist works with the family to identify any patterns of behavior or communication that may be contributing to the problem and to develop strategies to address these issues. This can involve resolving conflicts, improving communication, and building trust.

Family therapy can also help families to cope with the challenges of supporting the individual in their recovery. This can involve providing support and encouragement, helping the individual to find a support system, and dealing with the emotional and psychological effects of substance abuse. The therapist can help families to understand the importance of self-care and to find ways to support their own well-being while supporting the individual in their recovery.

In addition to family therapy, there are a number of other treatments that can be helpful for individuals struggling with SUD. These may include individual therapy, group therapy, medication-assisted treatment, and inpatient or outpatient treatment programs. The choice of treatment will depend on the individual's specific needs and the severity of their substance abuse.

Family therapy is a powerful tool in the treatment of SUD. It provides families with the tools and support they need to address the problem and to help the individual in their recovery. Family therapy is a collaborative and proactive approach that can help to rebuild relationships, improve communication, and promote a more positive and supportive environment for the individual and the family.

Motivational Interviewing for Family Members

Motivational Interviewing (MI) is a client-centered therapeutic approach that is commonly used by counselors to help individuals overcome addiction and SUDs. This approach can also be applied to family members of those with SUDs, and it can be highly effective in encouraging change and promoting recovery. MI is based on the principles of motivational psychology and seeks to enhance intrinsic motivation to change through effective communication and rapport-building. This approach is focused on eliciting change talk, which refers to statements that express a person's desire, ability, and reasons to change.

One of the key principles of MI is to respect the client's autonomy and decision-making process. This agrees with the Christian concept of free-will. This means that the therapist must avoid imposing their own values and beliefs on the client, and instead seek to understand the client's perspective and help them find their own motivations to change. This approach emphasizes the importance of creating a non-judgmental and empathetic environment that is supportive of the client's journey to recovery.

Family members of individuals with SUDs can play a crucial role in supporting their loved one's recovery, and MI can help them to effectively communicate with their loved one and encourage them to seek help. Family members often struggle with feelings of guilt, shame, anger, and frustration in response to their loved one's substance abuse, and MI can help them to navigate these feelings in a healthy and constructive way. This approach encourages family members to express their concerns and feelings in a non-confrontational and supportive manner, which can help to foster open and honest communication and promote a positive family dynamic.

MI also helps family members to understand the process of addiction and SUDs, which can reduce their stress and anxiety levels and improve their overall mental health. This approach can help family members to develop a deeper understanding of their loved one's situation, which can increase their empathy and compassion and reduce feelings of blame and resentment. This understanding can also help family members to identify their own needs and develop coping strategies to support their loved one's recovery.

Family Support Groups

Family support groups are gatherings of families and loved ones of individuals who struggle with SUDs. These groups provide a safe and supportive space for family members to connect with others who understand the challenges and emotions they are facing. Family support groups are designed to offer education, resources, and a supportive community to help families cope with the impact of SUDs on their lives.

Participating in a family support group can help family members to reduce feelings of isolation, guilt, and shame that often accompany a loved one's SUD. These groups provide a sense of belonging and understanding that can help to reduce stress and promote emotional well-being. Family support groups also provide opportunities for families to share their experiences and provide support to one another, which can help to build resilience and increase their ability to cope with the challenges of SUDs.

Family support groups also provide educational resources and information about SUDs and addiction, including the causes, symptoms, and effective treatments. This information can help family members to better understand their loved one's condition and provide them with the tools they need to support their loved one's recovery. Family support groups also offer resources and referrals to addiction treatment and recovery services, which can be especially important for families who are struggling to find appropriate treatment options for their loved one.

Additionally, family support groups can help families to identify and manage the impact of SUDs on their own lives. Family members may struggle with feelings of anger, guilt, and frustration, and a support group can help them to learn healthy coping strategies and develop a positive outlook. Family support groups can also help families to recognize the importance of self-care and support their own physical and emotional well-being.

Family support groups play a crucial role in supporting families affected by SUDs. These groups provide a safe and supportive community, education and resources, and opportunities for families to connect with others who understand their experiences. Family support groups can help families to cope with the impact of SUDs on their lives, develop healthy coping strategies, and support their loved one's recovery.

Coping with SUDs as a Family Member

Dealing with Denial and Resistance

Dealing with denial and resistance is a common challenge for families trying to help a loved one who struggles with SUD. Substance abuse can be difficult for the individual to acknowledge, and they may resist seeking help or engaging in treatment. Family members may feel frustrated and overwhelmed by the denial and resistance, and may struggle with how to support their loved one.

The first step in dealing with a loved one's denial can involve recognizing that their denial and resistance are normal parts of the addiction cycle. Substance use disorder is a complex condition that can distort a person's perception of reality, making it challenging for them to see the negative effects of their drug use. It's essential to respond with patience, compassion, and the love of Christ, avoiding feelings of frustration or anger towards a loved one's denial. By showing unconditional love and support, a Christian can provide a safe and secure environment for their loved one to overcome denial and resistance and move towards recovery.

One effective approach to dealing with denial and resistance is motivational interviewing. Motivational interviewing is a client-centered, non-confrontational approach to counseling that helps individuals to identify their own motivations for change and to build their own internal motivation to seek help. This approach can be especially effective for family members who are trying to help a loved one who is in denial about their SUD.

Another effective approach is to educate family members about the realities of SUD and the importance of seeking treatment. Family members can share information and resources with their loved one, and offer their support and encouragement for seeking help. They can also model healthy behaviors and lead by example, demonstrating the positive effects of recovery and the importance of self-care.

Family members who are impacted by a loved one's SUD face a unique set of challenges. Substance abuse can put a great deal of strain on relationships and cause conflict within families, leading to feelings of anger, guilt, and shame. In such situations, it is important for family members to set boundaries and practice self-care in order to maintain their own mental and emotional well-being.

This means taking the time to engage in activities that bring a sense of calm and balance to one's life, such as prayer, exercise, and hobbies. It may also mean avoiding enabling behaviors, such as covering for a loved one or making excuses for their substance use, which can perpetuate the problem. Unconditional love is also practicing "tough love" by not giving money to a loved one when you believe they will use it to buy more drugs, or gently but firmly denying them the ability to acquire their drug of choice. They won't like the word "no" but eventually they will appreciate the love you show in how you demonstrate it.

It's important for family members to understand that they are not responsible for their loved one's SUD, but they can play a role in their recovery. By taking care of themselves, setting boundaries, and seeking support from friends, family members can play an important role in helping their loved one towards recovery. In addition, family members can seek out family support groups, therapy or counseling to help them process their emotions and develop coping strategies for dealing with the challenges of a loved one's SUD.

Dealing with denial and resistance is a common challenge for families trying to help a loved one who struggles with SUD. Effective strategies for dealing with denial and resistance include motivational interviewing, education and resources, setting boundaries, and maintaining self-care. By understanding the realities of SUD and the importance of seeking treatment, families can help their loved one to overcome denial and resistance, and support their journey to recovery.

Addressing Codependency and Enabling Behaviors

Addressing codependency and enabling behaviors is a crucial aspect of the recovery process for families affected by SUD. Codependency refers to a pattern of behavior where a person enables another person's substance abuse by providing emotional or financial support, making excuses for their behavior, or covering up for them. This pattern of behavior often stems from a desire to help, but in reality, it only serves to enable the substance abuse and prevent the person from seeking help.

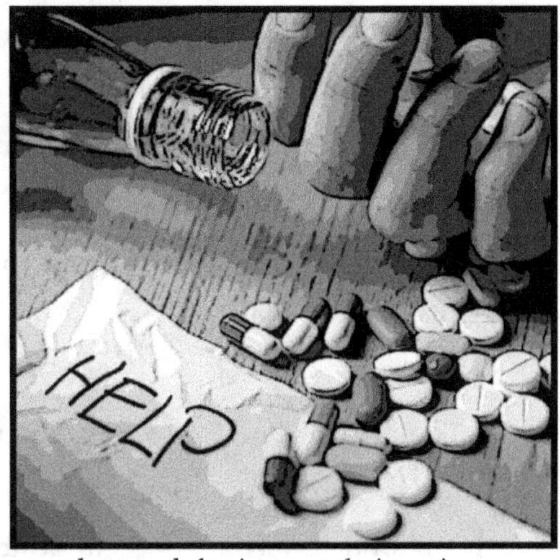

Enabling behaviors can take many forms, including financial support for the substance abuse, making excuses for the person's behavior, or covering up for them. These behaviors can be well-intentioned, but they ultimately reinforce the substance use and make it harder for the person to recognize the need for help.

In order to break the cycle of codependency and enabling behaviors, family members need to understand the impact their actions have on the person's SUD. This means setting clear boundaries, such as no longer providing financial support for the substance abuse, and refusing to cover up or make excuses for their behavior.

It's also important for family members to seek support and counseling to address their own emotional needs and learn healthy coping strategies. This can help them develop a sense of self-care and avoid becoming overwhelmed by the stress of their loved one's SUD. Seek out the support of your pastor or a friend at church. By setting clear boundaries, seeking support, and engaging in self-care, family members can play an important role in helping their loved one towards recovery and finding a healthier, happier future for themselves and their loved one.

Self-Care for Family Members

Self-care is an essential aspect of the recovery process for family members affected by a loved one's SUD. Caring for a loved one with SUD can be emotionally draining, and it is important for family members to prioritize their own well-being in order to provide the best support possible.

Making and IMPACT

Here are some ways family members can prioritize self-care:

- Practice stress management techniques: Substance use disorder can bring a lot of stress into a family's life, and it is important to find ways to manage this stress. This may include practices such as mindfulness, exercise, or therapy.

- Seek support from others: Support from friends, family, pastors, or a support group or connection group at church can help family members feel less isolated and better equipped to handle the challenges of caring for a loved one with SUD.

- Take time for yourself: Making time for activities you enjoy, such as hobbies or spending time with friends, can help family members recharge and reduce stress.

- Set boundaries: Family members need to set boundaries in order to protect their own well-being. This may include setting limits on the amount of time and energy they devote to caring for their loved one, and avoiding enabling behaviors that may perpetuate the substance use.

- Seek professional help: Family members may also benefit from professional counseling or therapy to address the emotional toll of caring for a loved one with SUD.

- Take care of your physical health: Maintaining a healthy diet, getting enough sleep, and engaging in regular exercise are all important for overall health and well-being.

- Avoid shame and guilt: Family members should avoid feeling guilty or ashamed about their loved one's SUD. Substance use disorder is a complex medical condition, and no one is perfect.

Self-care is a critical aspect of the recovery process for family members affected by a loved one's SUD. By prioritizing their own well-being and seeking support from others, family members can provide the best possible support for their loved one on their journey to recovery. It is important to remember that everyone's journey is different, and what works for one family may not work for another. It is essential for family members to find a self-care plan that works for them and to be open to adjusting their approach as needed. With self-care and support, family members can find the strength and resilience they need to navigate this difficult and rewarding journey.

The Importance of Family Involvement

Family involvement in SUD treatment is crucial as family members can play a critical role in supporting the recovery process. Family involvement in treatment can provide a supportive environment for the individual with SUD, increase accountability, and improve treatment outcomes. Family members can also gain a better understanding of addiction and how to support their loved one during and after treatment.

Family involvement can take many forms, including family therapy, education about SUD and addiction, and participation in support groups. Family therapy can help family members work through any conflicts or tensions that may have arisen as a result of the SUD and improve communication within the family. Education about SUD can help family members understand the disease and its effects, as well as how to support their loved one in recovery.

Support groups, such as Al-Anon or Nar-Anon, can provide a space for family members to connect with others who have gone through similar experiences and to gain practical advice and support. Family members can also participate in the treatment process by helping their loved one find appropriate treatment options, attending family therapy sessions, and assisting with aftercare planning.

Involving families in treatment can also help reduce the stigma surrounding SUD and promote a positive recovery outcome. Family members can provide a network of support, encouragement, and accountability, which can help increase the likelihood of sustained recovery.

However, it is important for family members to remember to prioritize their own self-care and boundaries during the treatment process. If you wear yourself out supporting others, you won't be able to support yourself. SUDs can be emotionally taxing, and it is important for family members to attend to their own needs and well-being.

The Ongoing Nature of SUD and Family Life Issues

SUD is a chronic condition that affects not only the individual struggling with substance abuse but also their loved ones. Family life can be greatly impacted by the presence of substance abuse, and this impact can last long after treatment has ended. SUD is a dynamic condition that can recur over time, requiring ongoing support and intervention from family members.

Relapse is a common challenge in SUD treatment and can bring new and unexpected stress to family life. Family members may feel frustrated, helpless, or even resentful as they continue to support their loved one in their recovery journey. The effects of substance abuse can also linger long after sobriety has been achieved, leading to relationship issues, trauma, and residual emotional and behavioral problems.

In light of these challenges, it is essential that family members understand the ongoing nature of SUD and the ways in which it may impact their lives. Family members may need to continue to provide support, attend therapy or support groups, and participate in educational programs. Family  members may also need to adopt new coping mechanisms, communication strategies, and boundaries to address any lingering issues related to substance use.

Ultimately, the key to successfully addressing the ongoing nature of SUD and its impact on family life is to engage in a proactive, ongoing approach to support and recovery. This may involve ongoing therapy, support groups, and other forms of educational and therapeutic intervention. By approaching SUD and its impact on family life as a lifelong journey, family members can work together to help their loved one maintain sobriety and build a fulfilling, healthy life.

Encouragement for Families Affected by SUD

Families affected by SUD often experience feelings of frustration, guilt, and shame. It is important for these families to receive encouragement and support in their journey towards healing and recovery. Family members can provide emotional support to each other and work together to help the individual struggling with substance use to seek treatment. Encouragement can also come from support groups, healthcare professionals, and peer mentorship programs.

Encouragement can take many forms, from providing practical assistance to offering words of comfort and reassurance. Families should be encouraged to take care of their own well-being, both physically and mentally, as this is essential for their ability to provide effective support to their loved one. They should also be encouraged to recognize their own strengths and limitations, and seek support from outside sources when necessary.

It is important to recognize that the journey towards recovery from SUD is a long-term process and that setbacks are a normal part of the process. Family members should be encouraged to have patience and persistence, and to not give up hope. They should be reminded that recovery is a process and that success can be achieved through consistent effort and support.

Encouragement can also come in the form of education and resources. Family members can be provided with information on SUD, its causes and effects, and available treatment options. They can also be connected with resources such as support groups and community-based programs to help them navigate this difficult journey.

Families affected by SUD need encouragement and support to help their loved one achieve recovery and to manage their own emotions and challenges. Encouragement can come from many sources, including family members, healthcare professionals, peer mentorship programs, and support groups. By providing encouragement and resources, families can help to break the cycle of SUD and achieve a brighter future for themselves and their loved one.

Understanding the Process of Change

We know that the journey of change can be challenging and complex, often requiring individuals to disrupt their sense of balance or stability. Resistance to change may arise due to various reasons, including fear of the unknown, a sense of loss of control, or a belief that making changes is impossible. But we know that all things are possible with God.

In therapy, both the therapist and the client share the responsibility to work together to address and overcome resistance to change. As Christians, we believe that God is with us throughout this process and can provide us with strength and guidance. Through prayer and seeking wisdom from God's Word, we can find the courage to overcome any resistance to change.

By working together, the therapist and the client can identify and address the root causes of resistance and develop strategies to overcome them. This may involve setting small, achievable goals, practicing self-compassion, and celebrating progress along the way. With the support of the therapist, the love of Christ, and the power of prayer, individuals can embrace change and find hope and healing on their journey of recovery.

The Story of John and Penny

In their marriage, John and Penny enjoyed a comfortable and content life. However, when a storm arrived, John was reminded of a problem he had ignored - a leak in their roof. The leak threatened to disrupt their sense of comfort and stability, but John had fallen into a pattern of complacency and ignored the issue.

It was only when Penny brought the problem to John's attention that he realized the seriousness of the situation. Although he was initially resistant to take action, Penny's persistence, memories of past storms, and the desire to avoid further discomfort motivated him to find a solution. With limited knowledge of roof repair, John sought advice from a salesperson named Steve, who recommended more expensive 20-year shingles.

Although John was initially hesitant, he ultimately trusted Steve's expertise and purchased the product. After successfully repairing the roof, John and Penny were able to return to their comfortable life. This experience taught them the importance of addressing problems before they become more severe and the value of seeking advice from trusted sources.

As a Christian couple, they also learned the importance of relying on their faith in God during difficult times. Through prayer and trust in God's guidance, they were able to navigate the storm and find a solution to their problem. They also realized the importance of supporting each other during times of change and disruption, and the value of seeking guidance from trusted members of their community.

Ultimately, John and Penny's experience taught them the importance of taking action in the face of change and disruption, and the value of seeking advice and support from trusted sources. By relying on their faith and the support of their community, they were able to overcome their challenges and find peace in the midst of the storm.

Change is Uncomfortable

The process of change can be a challenging one for many individuals as it often involves stepping out of one's comfort zone and embracing the unknown. This natural reluctance to change is driven by our tendency to cling to familiar patterns and habits, even if they may be harmful to our well-being. Additionally, conflicting beliefs and values can lead to psychological distress and further resistance to change.

In the context of drug addiction, this resistance can be especially pronounced, as individuals may have become dependent on the temporary pleasure that drugs provide. However, it is important to recognize that there is more to life than this temporary pleasure, and that progress towards a clean and sober lifestyle is both possible and necessary for personal growth and well-being.

Counseling can play a crucial role in facilitating change, but it is important to understand that the therapist is not the sole solution. Rather, they serve as a guide, providing the client with the tools and support necessary to overcome their addiction and maintain sobriety. This may involve a combination of therapy, medication, and support from friends and family, as addiction is a complex issue that requires a multidisciplinary approach.

The road to recovery is a long one, but it can be accomplished through a combination of hard work, discipline, and self-awareness. By changing irrational beliefs and thoughts through therapy, or by first modifying behaviors and gradually adapting beliefs, it is possible to overcome the temptations of drug use and maintain a clean and healthy lifestyle.

Change can be difficult, but it is a crucial step in the path towards personal growth and well-being. With the right tools, support, and discipline, it is possible to overcome the temptations of drug use and maintain a clean and sober lifestyle.

Understanding the Progression of Drug Use

Cravings can be intense. The ability to accurately describe physical sensations, such as hunger, may become compromised for individuals who have used drugs for an extended period of time. This phenomenon, known as anhedonia, refers to the inability to experience pleasure or satisfaction from activities that would typically be enjoyable. As drug use continues, the brain's reward system becomes altered, leading to a decreased ability to experience pleasure from food and other activities.

Additionally, prolonged drug use can also lead to changes in appetite and metabolism, making it difficult for individuals to accurately gauge their hunger levels. Talk to your doctor or a dietitian. Establish a regular exercise routine, go for a hike, play with your children, and keep in physical shape. Through proper diet and exercise, the body and brain can be re-trained to normal levels. It is important for individuals who struggle with drug addiction to seek professional help in order to address these changes in their body and make progress in recovery.

Drug use can have a significant impact on the brain's pleasure pathway, also known as the Mesolimbic Dopaminergic Reward pathway system. This system is responsible for generating positive emotions in response to pleasurable stimuli such as eating or sex. However, certain drugs, such as Quaaludes, can disrupt this system by excessively stimulating the release of dopamine, leading to feelings of intense pleasure. Over time, this can lead to a reduction in the ability of normally pleasurable activities to elicit positive emotions, and instead, the individual may become increasingly dependent on drug use as the only source of pleasure. This phenomenon is known as drug-induced hi-jacking of the pleasure pathway, and it can be a powerful driver of addiction. Furthermore, as the brain's reward system is disrupted, it can also lead to negative consequences, such as the decreased ability to feel pleasure from natural rewards and an increased risk of addiction.

The human body has a physiological response to drugs, leading to a craving similar to the craving for food or sex. Substance abuse has a significant impact on the brain, causing it to perceive the drug as a necessity rather than a preference. This physiological response is a normal part of recovery and should not be viewed as a setback.

It is important to acknowledge that individuals who struggle with addiction are not entirely in control of their actions. The brain, which has been altered by prolonged drug use, is only driven by the desire to consume more drugs, disregarding the negative consequences of drug use.

The phenomenon of "relapsing" refers to the reoccurrence of thoughts about the pleasurable effects of drugs, also known as "euphoric recall". This is a normal part of addiction and should not be discouraged. However, it is essential to keep in mind that individuals have the power to choose whether to give in to these thoughts or to overcome them. Maintain an awareness of the harmful effects of drug use and to resist the temptation to use drugs as a means of coping with life's challenges.

The average duration of craving is reported to be around 15-30 minutes. On a bad day, cravings might last about 45 minutes. Have a plan in place to manage cravings when they arise. There are several strategies that can be employed, such as seeking solitude, confiding in a trusted friend, or participating in group therapy sessions. The effectiveness of each strategy may vary depending on the individual's specific needs and circumstances.

It is also important for individuals to examine the reasons behind their drug use and the excuses they have used to justify it in the past. Such self-reflection can help individuals gain insight into their behavior and motivations. It is also important to acknowledge that excuses for drug use are not necessary and that there is no justification for substance abuse.

Ultimately, the decision to engage in drug use should not be made lightly, as it has serious implications for one's health and well-being. Substance abuse is never "ok." Instead, individuals should prioritize their health and well-being and seek support from friends, family, or healthcare professionals to help overcome their addiction.

The Progression Model

There is a debate about the nature of addiction, with some individuals viewing it as a disease, while others view it as problematic behavior. For the purposes of this publication, the Progression Model will be utilized as a framework for understanding addiction. This model posits that individuals engage in substance abuse as a means of altering their emotional state.

While the underlying motivation behind drug use may seem straightforward, the reality of addiction is complex and multi-faceted. Substance abuse has far-reaching consequences that can affect not only the individual but also their loved ones, community, and society as a whole. As such, IMPACT theory takes a comprehensive and nuanced approach when addressing addiction and substance abuse, treating the individual inside this entire system involving the counselor, client, and all those directly involved in his or her life.

The Progressive Model outlines six stages in the progression of substance abuse. These stages are:

1. Pre-experimental: This stage is characterized by an individual having limited or no exposure to drugs and limited knowledge about their effects.

2. Curious: At this stage, the individual begins to experiment with drugs and is curious about their effects.

3. Use at Parties: The individual begins to use drugs in social settings, such as parties.

4. On Weekdays: The frequency of drug use increases and begins to extend beyond weekend or party use, to include weekdays.

5. Alone: The individual begins to use drugs alone, potentially indicating a shift from social to problematic use.

6. All Day Any Day: Substance abuse becomes a daily occurrence and takes priority over other responsibilities and commitments.

It is important to note that the progression through these stages is not linear, and some individuals may progress through them more quickly or slowly than others. Additionally, the model is not intended to be prescriptive, and the experiences of individuals with substance abuse may vary. However, this model provides a framework for understanding the progression of addiction and can inform intervention and treatment strategies.

The Pre-experimental Stage of the Progressive Model refers to the time period before an individual decides to use drugs. This stage can be particularly vulnerable, as many individuals may start using drugs during a transitional period in life such as puberty. This can be a time of increased experimentation, but also a time when the individual is still protected by their parents. At times, the desire to fit in with a particular group of peers can lead to drug use, which can in turn lead to a detachment from traditional support systems such as family and teachers.

During the *Social/Recreational Use Stage*, individuals may begin to experience life problems such as a lack of belonging or inadequacy. This can be linked to developmental stages as described by Erik Erikson's stages of development. As one begins to use drugs to alleviate these problems, they may remember the efficiency and success of drugs in changing their feelings about the problem, even though drugs do not actually solve the problem. This can lead to an increased reliance on drugs, leading to further drug use to manage problems in their life.

Drug use affects the psychological well-being of an individual before physical health begins to deteriorate. People often rationalize and deny the problems in their family or work life caused by drugs, focusing only on the physical problems related to health. This is why it is crucial for individuals to be honest with themselves in recovery, and to understand the impact of drug use on their lives. The Progressive Model highlights the potential to intervene at different stages of drug use, and provides targeted methods of change depending on where the individual is in their progression toward addiction.

In the *Use at Parties Stage*, clients are now regularly using drugs. Drug use has already started to impact their life. The client needs to understand that the negative consequences of drug use are now more likely to happen. The counselor must now focus on educating the client on the short-term and long-term side effects of drug use. At this stage, the client is likely to be more receptive to the information being presented, as they are now starting to experience the negative consequences. This is also the stage where the client is more likely to seek help. At this point, the client needs to be taught how to recognize the triggers that lead to drug use. The client also needs to be taught how to reduce the harm associated with drug use and how to cope with the negative consequences of drug use. Outpatient counseling or an intensive outpatient program could be beneficial at this stage, as the client has started to experience negative consequences from their drug use but has not yet reached a stage where drug use has fully taken over their life.

In the *All Day Any Day Stage*, clients are now fully dependent on drugs. This stage is the end stage of drug use progression. The client needs to be taught how to manage drug use and avoid relapse. The focus needs to be on harm reduction, recovery skills, and relapse prevention strategies. The counselor should also focus on addressing the underlying problems that led to drug use in the first place. This stage requires the most intensive form of treatment, such as inpatient or residential treatment. The client needs to understand that recovery is a long-term process that requires ongoing support. This stage is the stage where the client is most likely to relapse, so the client needs to be taught how to recognize the warning signs of relapse and how to deal with these warning signs in a healthy and productive manner.

The stages of the Progression Model are essential tools for determining the appropriate interventions to provide clients in their journey towards recovery. However, it is crucial to note that these models should only serve as a guide and not as a definitive diagnosis. The effectiveness of the interventions lies in the accuracy of the client's diagnosis in these models.

The targeted interventions for a client in the contemplation stage who is curious about drugs will differ from those for a client in the same stage who is dependent on drugs. While both clients may be in the same stage of change, their experiences and motivations for seeking help are different, and the interventions should be tailored accordingly.

In formulating the client's learning experiences, the therapist should take into account the client's unique variables, including their life experiences, and professional assessment. The specific interventions that would be used are dependent on these factors and cannot be generalized. It is essential for the therapist to conduct a thorough assessment and design a tailored treatment plan for each individual client.

Tolerance: Needing a Substance Just to Feel Normal

Drug use can be a complex process that involves different phases. In the first phase, individuals may experience mood swings as they experiment with chemicals. They realize that these substances can provide temporary feelings of euphoria, which leads to an increase in drug use as they try to recreate and enhance these positive feelings. As drug use becomes a regular part of the individual's life, rules are established to govern their behavior, such as limiting drug use to weekends or social situations.

However, this phase marks the beginning of the individual's journey down the path of substance abuse and addiction. Over time, trust is established between the drug user and the substance as the individual becomes reliant on it to meet emotional needs that would normally be fulfilled through human relationships. It is important to note that the interventions provided to an individual during this stage must be carefully considered as they establish the foundation for the individual's understanding and relationship with drugs. Effective targeted interventions can help prevent the progression of drug use and potentially prevent addiction.

Eventually, the high after the first time using drugs is reduced, and the high becomes what used to be considered "normal." Users often chase the first high, never able to get it back again, and end up using drugs just to feel normal. The chart roughly illustrates this progression.

In phase two of substance use, the self-imposed rules developed in phase one begin to be disregarded. The user may view their substance use as being able to handle it at any time or feel justified in using it for emotional reasons. This leads to a loss of control over substance use and associated behaviors, which may conflict with their values and cause emotional pain. The resulting emotional disturbance and psychological distress go unresolved, leading to increased substance use in an effort to reach the desired state of "high". Substance use becomes the top priority in the person's life and lifestyle adjusts to revolve around obtaining and using the substance. However, the intense release of pleasurable chemicals during substance use results in feelings of depression post-use.

In the third phase of drug use, a new "normal" state is established for the substance user. The individual shifts from using drugs to achieve a state of euphoria to using them simply to feel "normal." Physical addiction may also occur at this stage. Substance use becomes a means of coping with the negative consequences of previous drug use episodes. The pursuit of the initial "high" is no longer attainable and the user develops a strong urge to continue using drugs just to maintain this new sense of normalcy.

WAKE UP: Targeted Interventions

Recognition of the necessity for change is a fundamental aspect of the journey toward change. Interventions can be utilized as a means of promoting awareness in individuals regarding their drug use as a concern. If an individual has a loved one who is struggling with drug use, an intervention may be crucial in guiding them toward recognizing the need for change and potentially saving their life. In instances where a client using drugs is in a state of denial, an intervention may assist in the realization of the need for change.

It is important to note that recognizing the need for change is a critical initial step in the change process. Interventions can be utilized as a means to bring individuals to the realization that their behavior is problematic, in this case, drug use. When a loved one is struggling with substance use, an intervention may be necessary to facilitate their understanding of the issue and potentially save their life. In situations where the individual is in denial about their drug use, an intervention may serve to bring awareness to the problem.

As an illustration of an intervention, a scenario involving a person with a door slamming habit can be discussed. The individual received a significant amount of pleasure from slamming doors, but it was disruptive and caused issues for others. A solution was sought to address this behavior and create a more positive environment for all parties involved.

An example of an intervention event was demonstrated in the case of a 17-year-old individual, who was in the "Identity vs Role Confusion" stage of Erikson's developmental stages and placed great importance on peer approval. The individual had a history of slamming doors in moments of conflict with their sibling, who would regularly transport them to and from high school. This behavior was deemed unacceptable, especially given the recent payment of the family's car. To address the issue, the sibling was instructed to lay on the horn loudly in front of the school each time the individual slammed the car door. This intervention was successful, as the individual ceased slamming doors after experiencing the negative consequences, which outweighed the perceived relief from the behavior.

The Iceberg Concept of Drugs

The drug use that can be seen is just the tip of the iceberg. The manifestation of drug use is a symptom of a deeper underlying issue (The Life Problem). It is important for individuals to assess and determine the root cause of their drug use, as it can differ from person to person. For

example, one individual may struggle with an unsatisfactory marriage, while another may struggle with feelings of dissatisfaction with their life. Until the root cause is addressed and addressed in a productive manner, it may continue to manifest in other negative behaviors, such as excessive gambling, overeating, or the use of pornography.

Therefore, it is crucial to identify the underlying issue, understand the need for change, and then take the necessary steps to achieve lasting, positive change in a pro-social manner. This may involve finding the motivation to change and striving towards a more fulfilling life.

The Formula for Change

As a counselor, my formula for changing a person's "substance use" lifestyle would include several key elements:

1. Assessment: It is essential to conduct a thorough assessment of the individual's drug use history, including patterns of use, triggers, and any underlying emotional or psychological issues that may be contributing to the problem.

2. Motivation: Identifying the individual's motivations for change is crucial. This can be done through goal-setting, exploring the pros and cons of continued drug use, and understanding the potential consequences of not changing.

3. Support: Having a support system in place, whether it be a therapist, peer support group, or family members, can be crucial in maintaining motivation and providing accountability throughout the process of change.

4. Coping skills: Teaching the individual coping skills and strategies to manage triggers and cravings is important in preventing relapse. This can include stress management techniques, mindfulness practices, and cognitive-behavioral therapy.

5. Relapse prevention: Planning for potential relapses and developing a relapse prevention plan can help the individual to anticipate and manage situations that may lead to a return to drug use.

6. Follow-up: Regular follow-up care is essential to ensure that the individual is maintaining their progress and addressing any challenges that may arise.

Breaking a drug use habit, (like any other habit) can be a difficult endeavor. However, by addressing the underlying reasons for the habit, setting clear goals, and having a support system in place, individuals can increase their chances of success.

Achieving some abstinence, or refraining from drug use for a certain period of time, is not the ultimate goal of the recovery process. Instead, it is a necessary step towards achieving sobriety, which involves experiencing life without the use of drugs and being able to fully feel the emotions that come with it. Resuming drug use after achieving sobriety can be detrimental, similar to jumping out of a plane without a parachute. It might be fun for a short time, but it never ends well.

Sobriety is a lifetime process that never ends. Always be vigilant. Never let a trigger end your achievements. The fun is temporary and not worth it.

The Keys to Recovery

 The path to recovery from drug addiction involves a multi-faceted approach that encompasses several key elements. The first key is an in-depth understanding and recognition of *the*

consequences of drug use. It is common for individuals to downplay the negative impact of drug use over time, but it is imperative to remember and reflect upon the detrimental effects that it has had on one's life. This is where 12-step support groups can be particularly helpful, as they provide a daily reminder of the consequences through new members and serve as a wake-up call for long-time members. To effectively address drug use, it is essential to fully grasp the magnitude of its consequences.

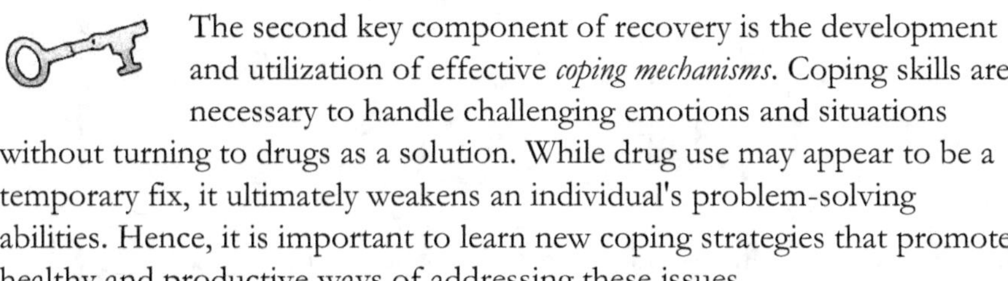

The second key component of recovery is the development and utilization of effective *coping mechanisms.* Coping skills are necessary to handle challenging emotions and situations without turning to drugs as a solution. While drug use may appear to be a temporary fix, it ultimately weakens an individual's problem-solving abilities. Hence, it is important to learn new coping strategies that promote healthy and productive ways of addressing these issues.

The third key part of a successful recovery journey is *effective communication.* Drug use can hinder the development of mature communication skills, making it essential to learn and practice effective communication in recovery. Communication plays a significant role in building and maintaining relationships, managing conflicts, and resolving issues.

Recovery requires a comprehensive approach that addresses the consequences of drug use, equips individuals with effective coping strategies, and fosters open and effective communication. Neglecting any of these elements can hinder progress in recovery. Consequences refer to the impact of drug use on an individual's life, and acknowledging and addressing these consequences is crucial for moving forward. Coping skills are the strategies used to manage challenging emotions and situations, while effective communication allows individuals in recovery to share their experiences and receive support and accountability from others. These three elements work together to ensure a successful life of recovery.

Steps in the Process

Life is an ever-evolving journey marked by continuous and progressive change. Change is not a one-time event, but rather a gradual and long-term process that involves a series of steps leading to positive or negative outcomes. These outcomes can then be evaluated and used to determine the next steps in the process of change.

The relationship between attitudes, behaviors, and consequences is a cyclical one, where attitudes drive behaviors, which in turn lead to consequences. To change negative attitudes and behaviors, it is necessary to associate the thought of engaging in negative behaviors with the negative consequences. This will shift the attitude and behavior, leading to long-term, positive, and desirable consequences that reinforce and sustain the change, reducing the risk of relapse.

However, it is crucial to recognize that these steps have varying meanings for different individuals and that a clear understanding of each step is essential for successfully navigating through the process of adaptive change. After evaluating the consequences, there may be the recognition of another need, triggering the process to start again. For instance, after successfully quitting marijuana use, an individual may then choose to focus on reducing alcohol use too. To gain a deeper understanding of this process, it is necessary to examine each step in detail.

Step 1: Recognizing the Need for Change

It is essential to identify the need for change in order to initiate the process of improvement or problem-solving. Change cannot happen unless the individual recognizes and acknowledges the need for it. The experience of pain, discomfort, or the lack of pleasure, as well as the potential for future pain or lack of pleasure, can serve as a catalyst for this realization. "There is an inherent need in all sentient beings to seek out positive and avoid negative stimuli…" (Volkow et al., 2019)

Consequences of previous behavior can also contribute to the feeling of pain or absence of pleasure. Education and personal experience shape our ability to predict future outcomes and guide our actions toward achieving the best results or pleasurable consequences. A wise individual will assess their current situation, make accurate predictions about their long-term future, alter the course of action accordingly, and strive for the best possible outcomes.

Interventions are a widely utilized strategy for facilitating the recognition of the need for change in individuals. However, it is important to note that interventions can be risky when the individuals involved do not have a strong bond, such as familial love. Family-led interventions can be effective but should be executed under the guidance of a trained intervention specialist. The use of a trained professional ensures that the intervention is carried out in a safe and effective manner. Furthermore, interventions should be done with the consent and willingness of the person who needs to change, to avoid resistance and further complications.

Realizing the existence of a problem is a crucial step in addressing and resolving it. However, this realization cannot occur without complete honesty and self-reflection on the part of the individual. Ego defense mechanisms, such as denial, minimization, and diversion, can prevent an individual from acknowledging and taking responsibility for their actions and the impact they have on their life and the lives of others. It is essential for the individual to recognize and overcome these defense mechanisms in order to make meaningful change.

Ultimately, you must take responsibility for your actions and the consequences you have on your own life and the lives of others.

Making and IMPACT

Consequences, whether positive or negative, can serve as a powerful motivator for change. However, it is important to note that a counselor, teacher, or parent cannot convince someone to change, it is a realization that the individual must come to on their own.

It is commonly acknowledged that individuals are often motivated to change when they are experiencing pain or discomfort. Do NOT deny a client their pain. To effectively facilitate change, it is important to first identify the current situation and determine whether or not the current trajectory will lead to further pain or discomfort. Additionally, it is essential to identify any unknown variables or potential future situations that may arise if no action is taken. By addressing these unknowns, individuals may be able to overcome the fear and uncertainty that often prevents them from making changes. Understanding the potential consequences of not taking action can serve as a powerful motivator for change. Therefore, it is imperative to evaluate the current situation and predict future outcomes in order to effectively facilitate change.

The drug use must stop, or the pain will continue. But pain is not the only possible consequence. Death is also a possible consequence. Because using or abstaining from some drugs can have deadly consequences, it is essential to seek the help of a trained professional or specialist in order to effectively navigate through the change process.

Once the need for change has been identified, developing a specific and actionable plan (with the help of a professional) is crucial. This plan should include identifying every step necessary to achieve the desired change and should take into account all possible resources and options. For example, if financial constraints are the root of the problem, creating a realistic budget and exploring alternative sources of income may be necessary.

Don't be afraid to ask for help. It is also important to seek guidance and support from trusted individuals, including family and friends, as well as professional help if necessary. In some cases, the need for change may be so great that seeking professional assistance is crucial for success. However, it is important to remember that fear should not prevent individuals from asking for help and support.

Ultimately, identifying the need for change and understanding the motivations behind it is essential for the successful implementation of change. By considering the current situation, potential consequences, and available resources, individuals can develop a comprehensive plan and take the necessary steps to achieve their goals. The love of family is a strong motivator – the number ONE motivator. And at the heart of Making an Impact, the primary message here is that "we're all in this together." If the client doesn't feel alone, they can find the strength to recover and support to continue successful, clean living.

The Body, Brain, and Pain

The brain also referred to as the mind, is where consciousness, perception, and logic exist. It is the physical part of the body that contains the mind, the consciousness, or the "soul." The brain is powerful and mysterious, capable of contemplating and pondering a wide range of processes, from involuntary processes such as breathing and hunger to cognitive processes such as writing or reading a book.

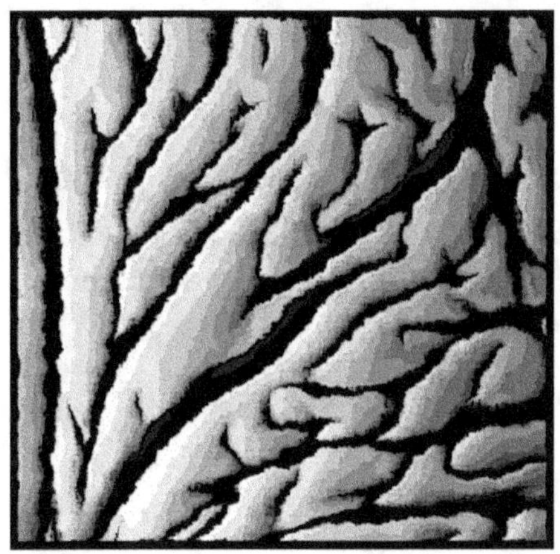

In the context of drug use, the mind plays a crucial role as thoughts and errors in thinking often precede the actions or behaviors leading to drug use. By recognizing and changing these thoughts, one can change their actions and behaviors. The mind is also where people remember the consequences of drug use and think through romanticizing self-talk, which can perpetuate the cycle of drug use.

The experience of pain is a complex phenomenon that encompasses both physical and emotional elements. It is important to understand the interconnectedness between the body, brain, and the experience of pain in order to effectively address the issue of drug use. These three interact to drive actions, also called behaviors.

It is widely acknowledged that individuals may have different perceptions of pain. While some may view it as a sign of vulnerability, it is essential to understand that pain serves as a critical warning signal that something is wrong within the body. Pain can manifest in various forms, including psychological, emotional, and physical pain.

While medication may offer temporary relief, it is important to avoid viewing the avoidance of pain as a privilege. A world without the experience of pain would present numerous challenges, such as a child not feeling the loss of a mother, or an individual with a broken leg continuing to walk on it, leading to further complications and increased pain. Therefore, it is crucial to address the root cause of the pain, rather than solely relying on medication for alleviation, as this approach could result in more severe issues.

Step 2: Finding the Motivation for Change

Identifying the motivations behind a change can provide the necessary drive to follow through with the transformation. Understanding the reasons for change is crucial, as simply recognizing a need for change is not enough to bring about lasting change.

Some individuals may question why change is necessary, as they may be content with the current state of affairs. However, it is important to consider the temporary satisfaction gained from maintaining the status quo and to recognize that this does not address underlying problems.

An analysis of the consequences of changing or not changing can also be useful. By considering the long-term effects of continued use, such as the impact on relationships, work, and overall well-being, individuals can make informed decisions about whether or not to make a change.

Motivation for behavior can often stem from two sources: discomfort avoidance and pleasure-seeking. Individuals may choose to avoid experiences that cause discomfort or pain, and instead, seek out situations that provide pleasure.

In the context of drug use, peer pressure or the desire for social acceptance may initially lead individuals to try drugs for the first time. Refusing the offer from friends or family may result in feelings of rejection, which can also be a source of discomfort or pain. On the other hand, gaining acceptance can provide pleasure and fulfillment, which are fundamental needs.

However, continued drug use may soon be driven by the pleasurable sensations the drugs provide, and evolve into addiction. Life without the drug can become painful, and the drug may be used to escape unpleasant experiences.

It's important to note that the right type of pain and pleasure can also be a strong motivator for not using drugs. By highlighting the negative consequences of drug use and focusing on the rewards of sobriety, individuals can be empowered to make healthier choices.

Positive motivations in life can come from various sources, but the love of family is often considered one of the most powerful. Family serves as a primary source of love, acceptance, and a sense of belonging for individuals.

Without the support and affection of family, individuals may struggle with psychological distress and maladjustment, potentially even leading to psychosis. However, with the presence of a supportive family, individuals can learn socially acceptable behaviors, develop their personalities through interactions with family members, and have their basic needs met.

There is also a strong desire for individuals to contribute to the cohesiveness of their family, by strengthening the bond between family members. The love for one's mother, in particular, has been recognized as a significant motivating force throughout history.

Determining the strength of motivation is crucial in assessing an individual's ability to bring about change. While some bodily functions, such as heartbeat and breathing, occur without conscious motivation, most behaviors, including drug use, have a strong underlying motivation.

Identifying personal motivations for change is an important step in the process of finding the strength to make meaningful changes. When motivations are strong, individuals have more compelling reasons to change and are more likely to successfully overcome any challenges or temptations to relapse.

The research findings demonstrate the crucial role of motivation in an individual's ability to effect change in their behavior. As suggested by Maslow and Stephens (2000), the strength of an individual's motivation to change can significantly impact their resolve to implement change in their lives. Personal motivation can be viewed as a driving force that can inspire individuals to take action towards their goals and can provide the necessary fuel to overcome obstacles and setbacks. Therefore, it is important for individuals to identify and understand their motivations to make lasting behavioral changes.

By harnessing the power of personal motivations, individuals can work towards achieving their desired outcomes, whether it be quitting a harmful habit, adopting healthier lifestyle choices, or pursuing new goals. For example, an individual who is motivated to quit smoking may set specific goals, such as reducing the number of cigarettes smoked per day or quitting altogether, and use their motivation to stay committed to their plan of action. As the individual experiences the benefits of their progress, their motivation can grow, creating a positive feedback loop that reinforces their commitment to change.

Assessing the strength of one's motivation is a crucial aspect of the change process. It is important to consider the potential consequences of not making changes, such as loss of job, family, and even life. While an individual may not initially place significant value on their own life, considering the impact on others can serve as a motivator.

As an individual begins to internalize the value of their relationships and the people in their life, their own self-worth and self-esteem will increase. This increase in self-esteem can provide the necessary strength to follow through with the process of change.

It is important to understand that valuing others and receiving value from them can have a positive impact on one's self-esteem and ultimately serve as a strong motivator for change.

Motivation is the drive to want more in life, and it is linked to factors such as meaning, family, acceptance, purpose, opportunity, society, employment, love, responsibility and respect. To succeed, one must plan their life, continue learning and education, and accept the challenge to overcome addiction. The motivation to change should come from a sense of importance placed on family, society, and personal growth through education and experience. Motivation, Opportunity, Responsibility, and Education are factors that can contribute to an individual's ability to succeed and make positive changes in their life.

Motivation is a powerful driving force that propels individuals towards their goals and aspirations. It is the inner desire and passion to achieve something meaningful and significant in one's life. The main thing that gives life meaning can vary from person to person, and it often involves factors such as personal values, relationships, career goals, spirituality, and self-improvement.

Opportunity refers to the range of possibilities and options available to an individual, both in the present and the future. It encompasses various aspects of life, including education, career, social connections, and personal growth. Recognizing and making the most of these opportunities can be a powerful motivator for change, as it enables individuals to create a path towards their desired outcomes.

Responsibility involves taking ownership of one's actions, behaviors, and relationships, and being accountable for their impact on oneself and others. Giving and receiving respect is an essential part of this responsibility, as it requires individuals to treat themselves and others with dignity, honesty, and fairness. By upholding these values, individuals can establish healthy and meaningful relationships that can serve as a source of motivation and support for change.

Education and past experiences can have a significant impact on an individual's future, as they shape one's perspectives, knowledge, and skills. Learning and growing from past experiences can provide valuable insights and tools for achieving personal and professional goals. Education, whether formal or informal, can also broaden horizons and open up new opportunities for growth and development, which can serve as powerful motivators for change.

Together, these factors can help individuals move forward and achieve their desired outcomes.

Top Ten Motivations

The motivation for change varies from person to person and is influenced by individual values and beliefs. It is important for individuals to identify what holds personal significance and drives their behavior change. This can aid in their journey to overcome drug addiction by providing them with a meaningful and effective source of motivation. The following are summarizations based on dozens of various client essays. These are the top ten reasons individuals listed for starting and stopping drug use.

Making and IMPACT

Top 10 motivations for clients to START using:

1. Pressure from drug-using family: Family members who use drugs can influence individuals to start or continue using drugs, either directly or indirectly. The pressure can come from the need to fit in, maintain relationships, or to avoid conflict.

2. Peer pressure from drug-using friends: Friends who use drugs can also be a significant source of pressure for individuals to start or continue using drugs. They may view drug use as normal behavior or view it as a bonding experience.

3. Sense of belonging to the crowd: Individuals may use drugs in order to feel like they belong to a specific social group or crowd. They may feel that using drugs is a way to fit in and be accepted.

4. Curiosity: Curiosity can drive individuals to try drugs. They may want to know what the experience is like or what effects it will have on them.

5. Feelings of fun, happiness, and euphoria: Drugs can produce feelings of happiness, fun, and euphoria. This can be a powerful motivator for individuals to continue using drugs.

6. Boredom: Boredom can drive individuals to try drugs. They may view drug use as a way to escape their boredom and experience something new.

7. Trying to fill a void: Individuals may use drugs as a way to fill a void in their lives. They may feel unfulfilled in other areas of their life and turn to drugs to fill that emptiness.

8. Accessibility: The availability of drugs can be a motivator for individuals to start or continue using drugs. The easier it is to obtain drugs, the more likely individuals are to use them.

9. Sex: Drugs can be associated with sexual experiences. Individuals may use drugs to enhance their sexual experiences or to feel more confident in sexual situations.

10. Fast money: Drug dealing can be a source of fast money for individuals. They may be motivated to sell drugs for financial gain, even if it means putting themselves in dangerous situations.

Top 10 motivations for clients to STOP using:

1. Incarceration: The possibility of being sentenced to prison and losing one's freedom as a consequence of drug use can be a powerful motivator to change. It can be an eye-opening experience that forces individuals to face the legal consequences of their actions and to consider the impact it has on their lives, freedom, and future prospects.

2. Death of a loved one: The loss of a family member or close friend due to drug-related issues can be a traumatic event that serves as a wake-up call for change. It can be a turning point in an individual's life, as they are forced to confront the reality of the harm that drug use can cause to those closest to them.

3. Loss of contact with family: The estrangement or disconnection from family members as a result of drug use can be a source of deep pain and regret. The sense of isolation and loneliness can be a driving force for individuals to change, as they come to realize the importance of their relationships with family and loved ones.

4. Loss of material possessions: The loss of a job, home, or other material possessions as a result of drug use can be a source of stress and fear. It can motivate individuals to change by forcing them to face the negative consequences of their drug use and to work toward stabilizing their lives and securing a better future.

5. Life became unmanageable: When drug uses spirals out of control, individuals may find their lives becoming increasingly chaotic and unmanageable. This can include financial difficulties, health problems, and relationship issues, among others. These mounting problems can motivate individuals to seek help and make changes to their drug-using behavior.

6. Tired of feeling worthless or like a failure: Individuals who struggle with feelings of worthlessness or failure can be motivated to change when they come to realize that drug use only exacerbates these negative feelings. Seeking help and making positive changes can help individuals regain a sense of control and purpose in their lives.

7. Burned out in drug-using lifestyle: Over time, individuals may become exhausted from the demands and stress of a drug-using lifestyle. This can include the physical and emotional toll, as well as the financial and social consequences. When individuals reach this point, they may be motivated to change in order to regain a sense of stability and well-being.

8. Future outlook: A focus on long-term goals and aspirations can be a powerful motivator for change. When individuals think about their future, they may be inspired to set aside drug use and pursue healthier, more fulfilling paths in life.

9. Life-threatening physical danger: The realization that drug use poses a threat to one's physical health and well-being can be a powerful motivator to change. This can include the fear of developing chronic health problems, overdose, or other life-threatening conditions.

10. Religious beliefs: For individuals with strong religious beliefs, the idea of engaging in behaviors that go against their faith can be a source of guilt and inner turmoil. This can be a motivator for change, as

individuals seek to align their actions with their religious values and principles.

Identifying the motivation to start using drugs is only the first step in avoiding relapse. Research shows that maintaining sobriety over time requires ongoing effort and support. It is important for the individual to develop a network of support, which may include friends, family, and mental health professionals. The support of others can provide encouragement, accountability, and a sense of belonging that can be critical to maintaining motivation.

In addition to support, developing healthy coping mechanisms is also essential. As discussed earlier, coping skills are sustainable and do not pose the same risks as drugs. These skills can include physical activities like exercise, meditation, deep breathing, and other relaxation techniques. Engaging in meaningful activities and spending time with loved ones can also provide a sense of purpose and fulfillment that can reduce the desire to use drugs.

It is important to note that relapse is common and does not signify failure. Rather, it is a natural part of the recovery process. Relapse can provide the individual with the opportunity to learn from their mistakes and develop better coping mechanisms. It is important for the individual to remain committed to their sobriety and seek help if they experience a relapse.

In summary, identifying the motivation to start and stop using drugs is an important step in maintaining sobriety. The individual can assess their motivation by reflecting on their triggers and motivations and by developing a support network and healthy coping mechanisms. With these tools, the individual can stay on the path toward recovery and achieve a fulfilling life without drugs.

Step 3: Using Education & Experience to Empower Change

Awareness can significantly influence an individual's perception and understanding of their circumstances, environment, and self. Perceptions are subjective interpretations of situations or individuals, which may be accurate or flawed, but to the individual, they become a valid representation. The acquisition of knowledge can change inaccurate perceptions and empower individuals to exert control and strength, and it can lead to positive changes. By recognizing the possibility of living a drug-free life and creating a plan to achieve it, individuals empower themselves to take the necessary steps towards recovery. Informed individuals are more likely to act on the information they have obtained. The elimination of drugs from one's life and maintaining sobriety enhances the likelihood of continued abstinence, and short-term success leads to long-term success.

An individual's attitudes are shaped by various factors throughout their life, such as parenting, social interactions, and life experiences at school, church, and work. Negative attitudes towards authority, for instance, can result from a lack of positive experiences with a strong father figure. Exposure to trauma, such as physical abuse, violence, childhood sexual abuse, and parental substance use, can also contribute to substance abuse. Research has established a strong correlation between exposure to violence and substance abuse (Logan et al., 2004). Personal traumatic experiences, such as physical abuse, violence, childhood sexual abuse, and parental substance use, have been identified as risk factors for substance abuse (McMurran et al., 2006; Marvin, 1997).

The link between trauma, including physical abuse, violence, childhood sexual abuse, and parental substance use, and substance abuse has been widely acknowledged. Substance use can serve as a coping mechanism for managing the pain associated with trauma, but it can quickly escalate into a problem in and of itself. Children of alcoholic parents are more prone to developing alcoholism as they tend to adopt their parent's attitudes and behaviors. While peer pressure and societal influences play a role in shaping attitudes towards substance use, parents hold a strong position of influence and can steer their children towards making healthy choices by demonstrating sobriety and setting a positive example through their actions.

Step 4: Changing Thinking Errors

It is imperative to understand the cognitive processes that influence behavior in order to successfully navigate the process of change. Thoughts play a crucial role in determining behavior, as individuals must comprehend their environment and the potential consequences of their actions. The mind-altering effects of drugs can significantly impact cognitive processes, particularly in the context of attaining sobriety.

Thoughts play a crucial role in shaping behavior. For a change in behavior to occur, a shift in perspective and thought process must first take place. This is because thoughts and emotions work together to inform decisions and drive action. People often use the phrase "I wasn't thinking" to excuse impulsive or unwise behavior, but it's important to note that behavior always stems from some form of thought.

It is a common misconception that our actions are solely a reaction to external stimuli. In actuality, a complex cognitive process takes place that influences our behavior. By examining this process, we can gain deeper insight into why we behave in certain ways. For example, what prompts our response when faced with different types of physical aggression, such as being slapped by a stranger or a family member? Understanding these nuances can shed light on our behavior.

The cognitive process begins with the perception of an image or event, which we view as our reality. Perception may not align with the actual reality, but it serves as our interpretation of it. What does the brain see? Is this image a vase, or it is 2 faces? In reality, it can be only one, but which one? The mental process then involves analyzing and making decisions based on this interpretation of the world  around us. We need more information to discover the truth. Be open to receive new information, and be ready to change what you perceive to be reality. Truth does not change, only our perception changes.

The process of listening is not just a physiological one, but an active cognitive one as well. Listening requires not only the ability to hear sounds but also being attentive and interpreting the perceived sounds. The development of language involves this cognitive process of listening, where infants must be able to differentiate between different sounds, pay attention to them, and interpret the meanings behind specific sounds. This highlights the importance of not just the physical capability of hearing, but the cognitive process of listening in the development of language.

Developing effective listening skills requires effort and practice. It is similar to learning a foreign language. Janusik (2007) highlights that successful conversational listening involves focusing on facts, inferences, and judgments presented, demonstrating active listening, exhibiting respect, identifying deception, determining motive or self-interest, and providing clear, positive feedback to the speaker. A response is also crucial in conversational listening (Janusik, 2007).

The use of drugs can disrupt an individual's perception of reality, leading to a distorted interpretation of the world around them. The initial euphoria experienced from drug use leads to an attempt to recreate that feeling with subsequent use. As a result, the importance placed on obtaining the drug becomes greater than anything else in life. Over time, the drug becomes a person's primary coping mechanism and everything else they once valued is replaced. This focus on the drug can lead to reckless or dangerous behavior, including criminal acts to obtain the substance. The individual's cognitive process becomes fixated on obtaining the drug, leading to impaired judgment and a disregard for the consequences of their actions.

The mind-altering properties of drugs have a direct impact on the cognitive processes involved in drug use. Upon first use, the unconscious part of the brain begins to influence the conscious mind, creating an intense memory of the experience. With repeated use, the neural pathways become ingrained, leading to a strong desire to use again. Understanding this process and recognizing cravings can empower an individual to consciously resist drug use, but often outside help is required to overcome the powerful desire to continue using.

Thinking Errors

Therapy posits that drug use stems from "thinking errors" that precede drug use behavior. Although it might not be politically correct to say so in today's society, these "thinking errors" are often referred to as "defects of character" or "shortcomings" in the 12 Steps program of Alcoholics Anonymous. The truth is these thinking errors refer to illogical thought patterns that lead to negative consequences and defeated behaviors.

For instance, if a person believes that they need drugs to cope with the pain of childhood abuse and sees themselves as a helpless victim, then they are engaging in the thinking error of being a victim. This kind of erroneous thinking may lead to statements like "I need drugs to overcome the pain of my abuse." On the other hand, if someone believes that they deserve anything they want and steal to obtain drugs, their thinking error might be "I deserve to have anything I need, so I will take what I want." A lack of time perspective may also lead to the desire for immediate gratification and the use of drugs as a quick source of profit and high feelings.

Making and IMPACT

Changing thought processes is a key component in changing behavior, but it's not an easy process. It requires effort, constant attention, awareness of thinking errors, correct thoughts, and practice.

Train Your Brain

Expanding on this concept, it is important to understand that our experiences, habits, and coping mechanisms shape the way we respond to emotions. Over time, our brain learns to associate certain behaviors with a reduction in emotional distress. This process is known as classical conditioning and it results in the development of automatic responses to triggers. For example, if we have been using drugs to cope with stress, our brains will have learned to associate drug use with relief. As a result, whenever we encounter stress, our brain will prompt us to use drugs, even if we are aware of the negative consequences. This highlights the power of the brain to learn and shape our behavior, and it also emphasizes the need to actively engage in rewiring our coping mechanisms to break the cycle of drug abuse.

Billy's scenario

Billy starts his baseball journey in Little League at a young age. (No issues present.) During adolescence, Billy faces some emotional distress. Fortunately, he joins an after-school program that helps him manage and release those feelings through positive social activities. (Some challenges experienced.) As Billy matures and enters the workforce, he faces common life challenges. He continues playing baseball on weekends, providing a physical outlet to release any built-up emotions. (A considerable number of challenges are present.)

Billy's brain has been conditioned over time through repeated exposure to baseball. As a result, baseball has become the primary coping mechanism for him, not through a deliberate decision, but rather through repeated experience. Every time Billy played baseball and used it to relieve his emotional stress, his brain associated the activity with relief and satisfaction. Thus, when faced with negative emotions, the brain naturally gravitates towards the coping mechanism it perceives as most successful in providing quick relief. This is because the brain is inherently programmed to meet its needs in the most efficient manner.

Here is another hypothetical situation. Remember as we move through this example, that people are creatures of perceived success:

Making and IMPACT

Cody's Scenario

The scenario involves Cody, who plays baseball with Billy on the high school team. Initially, Cody faces no issues. However, as he goes through adolescent growth and experiences emotional frustration, minor problems arise. At a party, Cody tries smoking weed and has a positive experience with little to no negative consequences. As Cody encounters normal life challenges, he continues to rely on weed as his preferred coping mechanism, leading to a rise in major problems.

When facing negative emotions, our brain naturally seeks out the most efficient solution to alleviate the discomfort. The choice of coping mechanism is therefore a crucial one as it will determine the level of relief and the length of time it takes to attain that relief.

On one hand, playing baseball with friends could provide a healthier and more long-lasting form of stress relief. This activity takes some time to set up, approximately three to four hours, but it has the potential to improve both physical and emotional well-being through exercise and social interaction.

On the other hand, turning to drugs such as marijuana may provide a quicker but short-lived form of relief. This approach takes only about thirty minutes to achieve the desired outcome, but it comes at the cost of potentially damaging one's health and well-being. Additionally, relying on drugs as a coping mechanism can lead to addiction and further problems down the line. The choice of coping mechanism should be considered carefully as it can have a significant impact on one's physical and emotional well-being.

Individuals must redirect their coping mechanisms when pursuing sobriety. The brain can be conditioned through consistent actions. Just as baseball and drug use were established through repetition as the go-to methods of handling unpleasant emotions, it's necessary to adopt a range of healthier coping skills and apply them regularly. Initially, these new coping methods may not provide the same level of satisfaction, but with persistence and repetition, the brain can be rewired as discussed previously. It's important to acknowledge that no coping strategy will match the intensity of drug use. Similar to how muscles can be strengthened through proper attention, training, and exercise, the mind too can heal with consistent care, training, and practice.

Making and IMPACT

Thinking Through

As shown in the diagram, thought #2 is "I want to get high," reflecting the established habit of using drugs as a default coping mechanism. This provides quick and reliable relief. After accepting the consequences of drug use, the client moves to thought #3 "consequences," leading to a healthier choice of thought #4 "I'll play video games." Although playing video games may not provide the same immediate relief as drug use, it does not have long-term harmful consequences. It's natural and normal to initially think about using drugs when facing a challenge, but it's important to consider alternative coping mechanisms.

Step 5: Understanding the Influence of Emotions

Emotions also play a crucial role, as feelings can interact with thoughts to influence decision-making and volition. Drug addiction is often a reflection of underlying emotional issues.

How Do Emotions Work?

Emotions are complex, multi-faceted experiences that are integral to our human existence. They are shaped by a multitude of factors, including neural processes, cognitive interpretations, physical sensations, and cultural backgrounds. As such, understanding the mechanisms that drive our emotional responses can have a profound impact on our overall well-being.

The process of experiencing emotions begins in the brain, where various neural pathways are activated in response to external stimuli. This process can be influenced by a number of factors, including genetics, past experiences, and environmental cues. The resulting emotional experience can range from positive feelings such as happiness and contentment to negative emotions like anger and sadness.

In addition to neural pathways, our thoughts and interpretations of events can also have a significant impact on our emotional experience. The same event may elicit different emotional responses from different individuals, based on their individual beliefs, values, and perceptions. Additionally, emotions are closely linked to physical sensations, with the release of hormones such as adrenaline and cortisol contributing to changes in heart rate, blood pressure, and other physiological responses. This interconnection between emotions and physical sensations is often referred to as the mind-body connection.

Making and IMPACT

Furthermore, our cultural backgrounds can also shape our emotional experiences, with different cultures placing varying levels of emphasis on the expression or suppression of certain emotions. Such cultural differences can impact how we experience and manage emotions in our daily lives.

Overall, emotions are a complex and dynamic aspect of the human experience that are shaped by a variety of factors. By gaining a deeper understanding of the mechanisms that drive our emotional responses, we can learn to manage our emotions in a healthy and productive way, leading to improved overall well-being.

The interplay between emotions and thoughts has a significant impact on decision-making, and can either boost one's confidence or lead to devastating consequences, such as considering suicide. Self-esteem is a crucial emotional factor in drug use.

Self-esteem, which is defined as one's overall evaluation of oneself, has been linked to various aspects of mental and physical well-being. Studies have shown that a healthy level of self-esteem is associated with higher levels of happiness, better coping mechanisms, and an increased sense of self-worth (Baumeister, Campbell, Krueger, & Vohs, 2003). On the other hand, low self-esteem can lead to feelings of worthlessness, anxiety, and depression, which may contribute to the development of addictive behaviors and the inability to make positive changes in one's life.

Alcoholics Anonymous recognizes the role that self-esteem plays in addiction recovery, particularly in acknowledging the feeling of powerlessness that arises from the inability to control one's drug use. However, it is important to note that individuals still have agency in their choices and can take control of their lives by making conscious decisions that align with their values and goals. In this way, self-esteem plays a crucial role in addiction recovery by providing individuals with the confidence and motivation to make positive changes in their lives.

Building self-esteem can be a challenging process, particularly for individuals struggling with addiction or other mental health issues. However, therapy and support groups like Alcoholics Anonymous can provide a safe and supportive environment for individuals to explore and address underlying issues that contribute to low self-esteem. By taking the time to reflect on one's values, strengths, and accomplishments, individuals can begin to develop a more positive and realistic self-image, which can lead to greater feelings of empowerment and control over one's life.

Making and IMPACT

Self-esteem plays a critical role in addiction recovery and an individual's ability to effect change in their life. By recognizing their agency and ability to make conscious choices, individuals can take control of their lives and work towards positive change. Seeking support from therapy and support groups can provide individuals with the tools and resources needed to build healthy self-esteem and achieve long-term recovery.

Acceptance of responsibility is crucial in addressing substance use. Taking ownership of one's substance use also implies taking responsibility for their recovery. It is important to note that an individual can only be accountable for things within their control, and in this context, the power to overcome substance use lies within. A lack of self-esteem can lead to feelings of helplessness, however, a positive self-esteem can empower an individual to overcome their substance use.

The connection between emotions and cravings is significant. The interplay between thoughts and emotions is regulated by the brain, and the impact of certain drugs on the brain leads to an amplification of thoughts and emotions. The saturation of dopamine and other neurotransmitters in neural pathways due to drug use is akin to a river flooding an area or a hillside being oversaturated with water, leading to potential harm. The flooding of drugs leads to chemical changes in the brain that alter the neural pathways. During drug use, the brain burns memories with increased intensity, based on the emotional intensity, creating deeply ingrained memories that can be difficult to forget.

Our brain has the remarkable ability to adapt and change over time, a process known as neuroplasticity. However, this adaptability can have negative consequences when intense, traumatic emotions become burned into our neural pathways. When things do not go as planned, the emotional impact can be powerful and long-lasting. A person who has experienced traumatic events may develop emotional responses that are triggered by everyday events or situations, leading to ongoing difficulties with emotional regulation. This phenomenon is known as emotional hijacking, in which emotions take over our thoughts and behaviors, often leading to impulsive and irrational decisions.

Psychological research has demonstrated the impact of past experiences and learned behaviors on our emotions. For example, a study conducted on a baby just a few months old who had not yet learned fear approached a venom-less snake with curiosity, whereas the experimenter cringed (APS, 2001). This shows how learned behaviors and past experiences shape our emotional responses to situations.

In addiction recovery, overcoming fear and other traumatic emotions stemming from drug use is essential for success. Emotional triumph, or the ability to manage and overcome negative emotions, is a key factor in achieving success in recovery. This involves learning to regulate emotions, building self-awareness, and identifying and changing negative thought patterns. By focusing on emotional triumph, individuals in recovery can break free from the emotional hijacking that often accompanies addiction and move toward a healthier, more fulfilling life.

It's crucial to understand the impact of emotions in drug use. Substance abuse is often a manifestation of emotional turmoil. While making responsible choices may seem simple in calm situations, it's much harder when emotions run high and cravings are intense. It's essential to address and overcome the emotional issues that fuel drug addiction to achieve lasting recovery and freedom from substance abuse.

Making and IMPACT

Emotional Baggage: The Zombie of Repressed Emotions

Repressed emotions can lead to negative outcomes such as unhealthy psychological distress, strained relationships, and the risk of relapse. Individuals in recovery must learn how to express their feelings in a healthy and productive manner, as this can prevent the build-up of unresolved emotions and the negative consequences that may arise. The words of Sigmund Freud, "Unexpressed emotions never die. They are buried alive and will come forth later in uglier ways," serve as a poignant reminder of the importance of effective communication in preventing negative outcomes.

Everyone has emotional baggage, but substance users often have a larger share of baggage that has not been dealt with – only repressed by drugs. In recovery, individuals should focus on developing pro-social coping skills, such as effective communication, instead of relying on substances to manage their emotions. Coping skills not only help to prevent the build-up of unresolved emotions, but also promote healthy relationships and a sense of personal growth and well-being.

How Do Drugs Make You Feel?

It is crucial to acknowledge the emotions associated with substance use. Paying attention to how one feels when under the influence of drugs or after the effects have worn off can provide valuable insight into the reasons for drug use in the first place. For example, if an individual reports feeling powerful when using cocaine, it may indicate that they have a low sense of self-worth and use the drug to compensate.

Similarly, feeling connected with friends when using marijuana may suggest the individual has difficulty with intimacy, possibly due to past experiences or low self-confidence, and uses drugs as a means to escape this fear. These emotions and experiences should be carefully examined to understand the root problem behind substance use.

Making and IMPACT

It is also important to consider how one feels when not using drugs. The difference between these two emotions can provide further insight into the relationship between drug use and the individual's underlying emotional struggles.

It is recommended to take the time to reflect on these questions and examine one's drug use in the same manner as these examples to gain a deeper understanding of their relationship with substances.

Using to Feel Normal

The use of drugs to feel "normal" is a common experience among drug users, as drugs can produce an intense euphoria in the beginning but eventually lead to a state of dependence and tolerance, requiring larger quantities or purer forms of the drug to achieve the same effect. This can be observed in the long-term use of tobacco and heroin, where users initially experience discomfort but eventually develop a learned behavior that provides relief and comfort. However, cessation of drug use can result in withdrawal symptoms, causing users to feel a strong urge to use again.

In recovery, it's not uncommon for individuals to experience dreams about drug use, as the body yearns for the experience. However, it's important to use logic and think about the consequences of drug use, seek help, and communicate feelings with a trusted friend or professional. Sigmund Freud believed that dreams are a manifestation of our desires, but in the case of drug use, it's important to remember that the body desires drugs, but individuals have the power to make a conscious, informed decision.

The Process of Joy

Joy is a complex emotional state that involves physiological, cognitive, and environmental factors. The experience of joy is marked by feelings of happiness, contentment, and fulfillment, and is triggered by positive events such as the attainment of a goal or the presence of loved ones. Physiologically, joy is linked to the activation of certain areas of the brain and the release of neurotransmitters that bind to receptors in the brain and activate the reward system. The cognitive and environmental factors that influence joy include an individual's outlook and perception of events and their relationships with others.

Using drugs to achieve joy is a dangerous process that can lead to addiction, physical and mental health problems, and damage to relationships and overall well-being. The use of drugs alters the brain's neurotransmitter systems, leading to an altered mood and emotional state. However, the use of drugs can also lead to involuntary stimulation of the brain, causing cravings and ultimately leading to relapse.

Support groups like Alcoholics Anonymous and Narcotics Anonymous can play an important role in promoting healthier approaches to addiction and maintaining sobriety. These groups provide a sense of community and understanding, which can be critical in the journey toward recovery. It is important to seek out positive and healthy ways to achieve joy and fulfillment, rather than relying on drugs, which can have severe consequences.

The avoidance of pain is a common theme in contemporary society, where pharmaceutical drugs are often seen as the solution to emotional and physical pain. However, this approach undermines the importance of pain in character development and can lead to the perpetuation of destructive behavior. While pain should not be sought out unnecessarily, it is a natural part of the human experience and serves an essential role in growth and learning from mistakes. In the case of inmates serving time in prison, pain is intended to serve as a motivator for change, but the overreliance on pain-relieving drugs can hinder personal growth and accountability.

The enabling behavior of loved ones, such as parents who provide monetary support for drug use, can also contribute to the avoidance of pain and hinder personal growth. This avoidance of consequences can lead to a lack of motivation for change and perpetuate destructive behavior. Furthermore, the overreliance on pain-relieving drugs is often driven by pharmaceutical companies and a lenient justice system.

It is important to note that there are individuals who genuinely require medication to manage their symptoms, but relying on drugs to avoid consequences or escape reality is not a sustainable solution. Acknowledging the role of pain in personal growth and taking accountability for one's actions is a necessary step in promoting positive change and well-being.

The Pain & Pleasure Cycle

The Pain & Pleasure Cycle is a well-known concept in the field of substance abuse counseling that explains the relationship between the pleasure associated with drug use and the subsequent pain and negative consequences that can arise from continued use. The initial experience of pleasure or ecstasy that is associated with drug use often motivates individuals to continue using drugs in an attempt to recapture the initial high, even though the pleasure derived from drug use decreases as the cycle continues. This cycle typically starts with experimentation, driven by curiosity or the influence of substance-using peers. As individuals face challenges in their daily lives, such as not fitting in with a particular group or feeling bored, their brain can be rewired to perceive drug use as a coping mechanism that provides pleasure and relief. However, as the cycle continues, the negative consequences and pain associated with drug use increase, making it imperative to break the cycle to avoid the potential destruction and death that can result from continued drug use.

The R.O.A.R. (Rules of Addiction Recovery) provide a comprehensive framework for understanding the process of addiction recovery.

- The cessation of drug use is the starting point for recovery. It is often necessary for an individual to experience the negative consequences of excessive drug use before they can commit to recovery.

- The primary goal of recovery is to stop using drugs, which must take precedence over all other considerations, including friends, employment, and family.

- Individuals will only make changes if they truly want to.

- The motivation for change must come from within, rather than being driven by external factors such as family.

- Developing healthy coping mechanisms is crucial for recovery, as it helps to fill the void left by drugs.

- The cost of drug use, both monetary and emotional, must be acknowledged and understood.

- The motivation for change must be internalized, rather than being solely driven by external consequences such as problems with family, employment, or the law.

- Excuses for drug use can be found everywhere, and it is important to recognize that individuals will only make changes if they truly want to.

- Cravings are a normal part of the recovery process and can be managed by waiting them out.

- The most effective treatment is often the accumulation of negative consequences.

- Understanding the initial motivation behind drug use can aid in the recovery process.

The researchers have noted that some individuals who participate in substance abuse treatment programs, such as the Pre-Release Substance Abuse Treatment Program (PRSAP), may not have a genuine motivation for recovery. Rather, they may participate in the program for reasons such as early release from prison, appeasing family members, or improving their criminal record. While the prospect of early release may motivate individuals to complete the program, it may not result in lasting behavioral change.

This lack of genuine motivation for recovery highlights the importance of assessing an individual's true desire for change when entering a treatment program. It is crucial to distinguish between reasons and excuses that individuals may give to explain their behavior. While it may seem logical for someone to engage in illegal activities to provide for their family, it is essential to acknowledge that many individuals support their families without resorting to such actions.

Furthermore, the lack of genuine motivation for recovery can lead to unintended consequences, such as a higher recidivism rate among those who are released from PRSAP prisons. The program screens for past drug use but does not assess an individual's willingness to change, which can be a significant factor in long-term success.

The Story of Martin

Once upon a time, in the small town of Riverdale, there lived a man named Martin. Martin was no ordinary man, for he had found himself in quite the predicament. You see, Martin had been thrown behind bars for selling illegal drugs to make ends meet for his family.

Now, when Martin was asked about his heinous crime, he simply replied, "I was providing for my family." Martin believed that he had a valid excuse for breaking the law. But the townspeople, oh they were not convinced.

They knew that Martin's justification was nothing more than a feeble attempt to defend his actions. For there were countless other individuals in the town who supported their families through legal means. They worked hard and struggled to make ends meet, but they did not resort to the unsavory tactics that Martin employed.

Martin's preacher who related this tale stressed that true change only comes from within. Martin and those like him would have to take responsibility for their actions and face the consequences of their decisions. They could not continue to blame their circumstances for their poor choices.

In the end, Martin was left to contemplate his misdeeds behind bars. His family suffered the consequences of his actions and the town moved on, wiser for the experience. And so, the tale of Martin came to a close, reminding us all that we are responsible for our own destiny, and that excuses only serve to shield us from the truth.

In the context of recovery, it is necessary to confront any excuses or justifications that an individual may have for their substance use. It is crucial to engage in an open and honest conversation with the person and highlight any discrepancies or weaknesses in their reasoning. While it is essential to approach the conversation in a non-judgmental and empathetic manner, it is also important to emphasize the consequences of continued substance use. In many cases, individuals who are resistant to recovery have not fully experienced the negative effects of their actions. By providing them with a clear understanding of these consequences, it may become evident that the temporary relief provided by substance use is not worth the long-term negative impact.

The most effective treatment for addiction often involves facing the consequences of one's actions, as this helps the individual realize the gravity of their problem. However, it is important to note that while these are general rules, there are always exceptions. Unfortunately, most people fall under these rules, and only a small minority can break these rules and still avoid drug use. The challenge is that most people hear stories about the minority group (who can break the rules without consequence) and believe they belong in that group. This idea can act as a gateway that repeatedly opens the door to drug use. Chances are, if you are reading this, you do not belong to the minority. By following the R.O.A.R. (the rules), you will not be tempted by rumors or misconceptions.

Are You a Man?

What does it mean to be a man? What kind of role model is your son seeking inspiration from? The concept of masculinity has been explored in numerous books and is portrayed differently in various media. For example, television often portrays men as cool, physically strong, and always ready for action. Each family also has its own definition of masculinity. William M. Struthers, in his book "Wired for Intimacy," presents the O'Neal model of masculinity which involves (1) a focus on independence and achievement, with efficient use of time and resources; (2) dominance in interactions with others, avoiding relationship styles perceived as feminine or implying homosexuality; and (3) rationality, with emotions suppressed or restricted.

When it comes to emotions, people may not always act rationally, and sometimes, outbursts are unavoidable. Despite societal and cultural expectations that men should suppress their emotions, it is natural for men to experience emotions and to express them through crying or yelling. Emotions are often taboo in society and are not well understood, much like drug use. Suppressing emotions can lead to a buildup of unresolved feelings, known as the Bottleneck Effect, and ignoring these emotions may cause further harm in the long run.

When hearing the term "bad emotions," common emotions that come to mind for many individuals include anger, anxiety, and sadness. These emotions are often considered "bad" because they are difficult to handle, but they are normal and are often necessary in certain situations. Men, in particular, may struggle to express these emotions due to societal expectations to suppress them or due to a lack of experience with emotional expression. It is important to recognize that everyone experiences these emotions, regardless of gender, and the key is to learn how to respond to and express them in a healthy manner.

Here's an example of a poor emotional reaction:

The following scenario exemplifies an unfavorable emotional response: Chris makes an insulting remark to Jack, leading to an escalating argument. This results in Chris physically assaulting Jack, to which Jack retaliates by striking back, leading to a physical altercation between the two.

Here's another example with a slightly improved response:

Mother: "Bob, why did you make that poor decision? Can't you see the consequences of your actions?"

Bob: "Whatever, it's not a big deal." (rude comment)

Mother: (slaps Bob across the face) "How dare you talk to me like that! I'm your mother and you will respect me."

Bob: (does not hit back) "I need some space. I'll be back later." (leaves)

This example highlights the importance of being able to make conscious decisions rather than simply reacting impulsively in fast-paced situations. If one were to act solely on instinct, they may have responded in the same physical manner as Jack and Chris did. This is particularly relevant in the context of drug recovery, as relapses may trigger thoughts of substance use. It is crucial to assess these thoughts and the potential consequences before acting on them. Take a look at this example:

Thinking through a Relapse Trigger: Jane, who is in recovery for marijuana addiction, is driving when she encounters a car emitting the familiar scent of marijuana. This triggers memories of her past use, a flash back about all the "good times" she had when she used to use marijuana, and a temptation to seek out the substance. However, she makes a conscious decision to resist the urge and maintain her sobriety, rather than acting impulsively on her craving.

It is a common reaction in American culture to cope with the loss of a loved one through excessive alcohol consumption. However, if we continually use alcohol as a means of avoiding grief, we may fall into a repetitive cycle of pain and relief through substance use for the rest of our life. As counselors, it is important to create a safe and supportive environment for clients to express their emotions. Suppressing emotions is a common cultural expectation for men, but it can hinder their ability to express themselves and be vulnerable. This lack of openness can become a barrier to recovery and emotional growth. Encouraging clients to freely express their feelings and emotions is a crucial aspect of promoting coping skills and preventing future relapses.

Making and IMPACT

Mankind's Misconception of Fear

In American society, there is a pervasive societal belief that vulnerability is a weakness and should be avoided, especially in the realm of emotions. This notion is particularly relevant when it comes to fear. However, it's essential to understand that courage is not the absence of fear, but rather the ability to confront and navigate through fear. The presence of fear is a normal and universal experience, but what sets individuals apart is their willingness to face their fears and work through them.

Fear is a natural and adaptive emotion that has kept us safe from harm throughout history. There is nothing wrong with being afraid of a snake or bear, but knowledge is even more powerful. Fear is often stigmatized as a negative or "bad" emotion, when in fact it can be a valuable source of information and a catalyst for growth and positive human development.

It is important for professionals to understand the role of fear in the lives of their clients and to create a safe, non-judgmental space where clients can express and explore their emotions. This is particularly relevant in recovery, as fear and other emotions can trigger relapses if not effectively addressed. By embracing vulnerability and facing fears, individuals can build resilience and prevent future relapse.

Being Uncomfortable with Yourself

It is a common observation that individuals who turn to substance abuse often lack a strong sense of self and struggle with the question of their identity. The pressure to conform to societal norms and the influence of peer groups can make it difficult for individuals to determine who they are as individuals. This can be particularly pronounced in youth, when the need for acceptance and belonging is at its peak.

In such scenarios, substance abuse can become a way of defining oneself. By aligning with a group that accepts and approves of drug use, individuals may feel a sense of validation and belonging. However, this is a dangerous trap as drug use becomes an integral part of their identity and self-worth, leading to a vicious cycle of substance abuse and further damage to their self-esteem.

Thus, it is imperative for individuals in recovery to work on developing a strong sense of self, beyond their drug use. This can be done through various self-discovery exercises, therapy, and by surrounding themselves with supportive and non-judgmental individuals. A healthy sense of self can help individuals in recovery break free from the negative influences of their past and build a fulfilling and drug-free life.

Instead of facing their emotions and developing their sense of self, many individuals who struggle with drug use resort to numbing their feelings through substance abuse. This is a temporary and unsustainable solution that prevents them from gaining a deeper understanding of who they are as a person.

Experiencing life's challenges, both good and bad, is crucial for personal growth. This includes handling uncomfortable situations such as starting a conversation, being still and dealing with silence, or even taking a slow dance. By facing these odd moments, individuals learn how to navigate new experiences and eventually break through their shyness. This is the first step towards becoming a unique and self-assured individual.

It is unrealistic to expect to avoid unpleasant emotions entirely, and drugs only serve to further distance an individual from their true self. Instead, recovery requires embracing these challenging experiences and learning to cope with them in a healthy and productive way. "Things are going to get worse before they get better" is a common phrase in the drug recovery process. By persevering through the difficult stages, individuals can eventually reach a place of lasting improvement.

The drug use can be seen as a manifestation of deeper issues, like the tip of an iceberg. The drug use is merely a symptom, just like a runny nose is a symptom of an infection. When the drugs are stopped, the underlying problem surfaces. For instance, consider John who started abusing drugs after having an affair at work. He used drugs to suppress the guilt he felt, but once he stopped taking the drugs, the guilt from the affair would come to the forefront.

Making and IMPACT

Drug users, like John, often struggle with life. They find it difficult to cope with the ups and downs of everyday emotions and find life overwhelming. The rollercoaster of emotions is the true "trip" and not just the experience of a drug-induced high. However, it is important for recovering drug users to understand that life does not magically become easy just because they are in sobriety. They will still face problems and frustrations, but they can choose to use it as an opportunity for growth or as a relapse trigger.

The use of drugs has been linked to a wide range of emotional states that are often considered "normal" for drug users. This fluctuation in emotions is in stark contrast to the more consistent and balanced emotional range experienced by non-drug users. This difference is a result of drugs altering the normal emotional state of a person, which can lead to significant changes in mood and behavior.

Address the underlying problems that lead to drug use rather than simply treating the symptoms with drugs. A more holistic approach that includes addressing the root cause of addiction, such as psychological or environmental factors, is crucial to successful recovery. This approach can help individuals to develop healthy coping mechanisms that enable them to manage and regulate their emotions without resorting to drug use.

Furthermore, emotions are not within our direct control, but they can be influenced by our thoughts and perceptions. Attempts to suppress or ignore emotions are often ineffective and can lead to negative consequences. Instead, individuals can learn to impact the way they feel by changing their thoughts and perspectives. This highlights the significance of our attitude and the power it holds in shaping the quality of our life experiences.

For example, by adopting a positive outlook, individuals can turn challenging situations into growth opportunities. In contrast, a negative outlook can amplify difficulties, leading to further emotional instability. Therefore, a critical component of successful recovery is helping individuals develop a positive attitude towards life. This includes learning to cope with the range of emotions that come with it.

Drug use can lead to a wide range of emotions, which underscores the importance of addressing the underlying problems that contribute to addiction. A holistic approach that includes developing healthy coping mechanisms and a positive outlook can help individuals to manage and regulate their emotions, leading to a more balanced and fulfilling life.

Step 6: Changing Perceptions and Attitudes

Also known as "Our Inner Eyes," perceptions are individual interpretations of reality. Because perception depends on an individual's location at the time, perceptions vary greatly and impact behavior and decision-making to varying degrees. How you perceive a situation is also called your attitude. Is your cup half full, or half empty? What's your outlook? One's outlook on life can also play a role in shaping behavior.

Perceptions Alter Decisions

The human brain is capable of understanding its environment by processing and interpreting sensory information. This includes our interpretation of events, people, situations, and even our own selves. Our perceptions and understanding of reality can be altered and improved through gaining knowledge and information. For example, an astronaut might initially believe that there is no air inside their spaceship, but upon receiving reliable information from their instruments or other astronauts, they can adjust their perception and remove their helmet with confidence. Similarly, having a better understanding of how our lives will change when we no longer depend on drugs can motivate us to overcome addiction, just like removing the helmet in the spaceship example.

Our current emotional state and the way we feel about ourselves and our surroundings can be influenced by our interpretation of events. Our interpretations of events, in turn, directly impact our decisions and actions. Whether or not we control our perception of events or if events themselves define our lives is a matter of perspective. While our actions and hard work can lead to positive outcomes such as praise, promotions, and a higher standard of living, external factors such as the global economy, inflation, and international job exports can also play a role in our outcomes.

In some cases, if we feel that we have done our best work but do not receive the recognition or promotion we feel we deserve, it is important to reflect on our perception of the situation. It may be that our interpretation of events is incorrect, and there could be other factors at play. On the other hand, if we do not perform well and do not receive recognition, this can serve as motivation to improve. However, it is important to be mindful of how we view the events and our perceptions of ourselves, as our outlook on the world can significantly impact our self-esteem and overall emotional well-being.

Attribution Styles

The perception of reality is subjective and unique to each individual. Our perspective and viewpoint on the causes of our problems greatly affect our ability to cope with stress, overcome obstacles, and live a drug-free life. An attribution style refers to the way in which we attribute the causes and consequences of our problems. This can range from viewing problems as internal and originating within ourselves, to viewing problems as external and originating from external factors.

Our attribution style can be categorized as *internal vs. external* attribution, *stable vs. unstable* and *global vs. specific*. For example, one may view the cause of a problem as unstable and specific to that particular situation, while another may view it as stable and having global impacts on their life. These attribution styles can be thought of as existing on a spectrum, but for simplicity, they can be viewed as dichotomous (having two sides).

These attribution styles are chosen for each problem that we encounter in life and can vary from situation to situation. By focusing on a specific attribution style, we can target specific areas for treatment and personal growth. Understanding our personal attribution style can help us understand the way we perceive and react to the challenges in our lives.

Internal / External

- Problems are caused by either Self or Others.

- Those with Internal attribution style view the cause of problems originating with the self or within the realm of one's self-control.

- Those with External attribution style view the causes of problems as other people, places, environments, genetics, and things outside of themselves or outside of their realm of control.

Internal attribution style means that individuals tend to attribute the causes of events to their own personal characteristics, such as abilities, personality traits, or intentions. This way of thinking suggests that if something goes wrong, it is because of something inherently wrong with the individual, such as lack of effort, ability, or being inherently flawed in some way.

External attribution style, on the other hand, means that individuals tend to attribute the causes of events to situational factors, such as the environment, other people's behavior, or luck. This way of thinking suggests that if something goes wrong, it is due to external factors beyond the individual's control, such as a difficult situation, someone else's behavior, or pure chance.

People can vary in the extent to which they use internal vs external attributions, and this can have a significant impact on their emotional and behavioral responses to events. For example, those who make internal attributions may be more likely to feel discouraged, while those who make external attributions may be more likely to feel encouraged.

Stable / Unstable.

- Problems are viewed as either Concrete or Changeable.

- Those with Stable attribution style view the cause and consequences of problems as never changing, concrete, and permanent. Things won't change.

- Those with Unstable attribution style view the cause and consequences of problems as changing, fluid, and flexible. Things will eventually change.

Stable attribution style refers to the belief that a person's behavior is a consistent, permanent part of their character or personality. In other words, if someone behaves a certain way, it is believed to be due to an underlying trait that they possess and that is unlikely to change.

Unstable attribution style, on the other hand, refers to the belief that a person's behavior is subject to change and is likely to be influenced by situational factors. In other words, if someone behaves a certain way, it is believed to be due to temporary circumstances, rather than an inherent part of their personality.

The stable vs unstable attribution style can have a significant impact on a person's emotions and behavior. For example, individuals who make stable attributions may be more likely to judge others harshly and hold grudges, while those who make unstable attributions may be more likely to forgive and let go of negative feelings.

Global / Specific

- Problems are viewed as either related to all other problems, obstacles, or difficulties, or unrelated to other problems.

- People with Global attribution style view all things as connected. One bad thing leads to another, and something bad will affect everything else in life.

- People with Specific attribution style view each event as unrelated to other events

Global attribution style refers to the belief that a person's behavior is due to broad, general causes that apply to all aspects of their life. For example, if someone is seen as being generally lazy, it is believed that their lack of effort applies to all areas of their life, such as work, school, and relationships.

Specific attribution style, on the other hand, refers to the belief that a person's behavior is due to specific causes that apply only to specific situations. For example, if someone is seen as being lazy in one particular situation, it is believed that this behavior is specific to that situation and does not reflect a general lack of effort.

The global vs specific attribution style can have a significant impact on how people perceive and respond to events. For example, those who make global attributions may be more likely to form negative stereotypes and generalize their negative feelings, while those who make specific attributions may be more likely to focus on specific behaviors and avoid making blanket judgments.

According to Rodriguez (2006), the external + unstable + specific attribution style is considered the preferred method for managing normal problems and stress during challenging times. Individuals with this style view the causes of problems as being external to themselves, such as other people, environments, or circumstances. They also view the causes and consequences of these problems as being flexible and capable of change. Furthermore, they perceive events and situations as being specific to the current event or situation, rather than part of a larger, overarching pattern. By viewing problems in this manner, individuals can avoid feeling overwhelmed by challenges that are outside of their control or related to an overwhelming chain of negative events.

It is important to note that the external attribution style may be effective for most individuals in normal circumstances, however, it may not be the preferred style for dealing with problems related to drug use, which is considered an extraordinary kind of problem. External attribution style is not the preferred style for dealing with drug users.

The internal attribution style is considered an effective approach for individuals who struggle with drug use. This style involves an examination of one's own perspective and views on their problems. While the initial use of drugs may have been influenced by external factors such as peer pressure, accessibility, or curiosity, it is important for drug users to recognize that their continued drug use is largely a result of their own choices and behavior.

Adopting an internal attribution style involves taking responsibility for one's own actions and recognizing that their drug use is a result of their own decisions and behaviors. This can help drug users to understand the role that they play in their own addiction and provide them with the motivation and empowerment to make changes and seek help. By recognizing that their drug use is a result of their own choices, drug users can also avoid feelings of victimhood and instead focus on taking control of their lives and seeking recovery.

While external factors may play a role in a person's initial drug use, continued drug use is often due to internal attributes. It is important to note that drug use does not define a person as "bad," as many individuals who would be considered "good" also struggle with drug addiction. To overcome this problem, an individual can adopt an external attribution style by removing themselves from the people, places, and circumstances that influence their drug use.

However, the ultimate choice to use or abstain from drugs lies with the individual, and this is where the internal attribution style comes into play. By recognizing that they have control over their own actions, individuals can empower themselves to make positive changes and take responsibility for their own recovery. It is important to note that external factors such as the environment or situation may influence a person to use drugs, but they do not have control over the individual. The decision to use drugs ultimately lies with the individual and they have the power to make positive changes in their life.

This implies that individuals have control over their self-perception and how they view their problems, as well as control over their own actions. While an individual may not always perceive themselves as being in control of certain situations and may believe that events in life happen randomly, it is possible for them to change their perspective. By becoming aware of their typical attribution style and making a conscious effort to shift their viewpoint, they can take control of their life, particularly in regards to their drug use.

View life as a series of events that are within one's control and to take responsibility for one's actions. By embracing this mindset, individuals can empower themselves to overcome addiction and maintain sobriety. Taking control of one's own life and embracing responsibility are key steps towards achieving a drug-free life.

Top Ten Sayings of Substance Users

1. I can't deal with life! The pain of my past made me the way I am today, and I can't deal with it without drugs.

2. I can't accomplish anything! I need drugs to survive.

3. I didn't do it, man, honestly! I'm innocent. Somebody else is to blame.

4. I need you. Really, I do. Just leave me alone. Even though I realize I need people and want to connect with you, I prefer to be alone and wallow in my self-pity.

5. You can't tell me what to do. I'm old enough to make my own decisions. I have the right to do anything I want.

6. I don't want to talk about it. Just let me cry. I'm so depressed I can't think straight.

7. Simple pleasures make me happy, like playing Xbox or watching TV. I just want to be happy. Just let me have my drugs and be happy.

8. Are you mad at me? I just want to be accepted. I can't help it if this drug has control of my life. Please accept me for who I am, and forget about the drugs.

9. Teens: "Live like there's no tomorrow!" We'll never get caught, so let's party hardy.

10. Adults: "Remember the good old days…" Relax and have a drink (or a little joint) because you only live once. This will help you remember the good times.

11. I'm having too much fun to stop now! "Crack is whack!" This feels fantastic. (No thought of consequences.)

12. Either you're for me or against me. Jesus said "don't judge, lest you be judged." You're a Christian – you're not supposed to judge me.

Okay, so there are twelve. It is not uncommon for individuals struggling with substance abuse to have similar thoughts and feelings as those expressed in the statements mentioned. In fact, even famous celebrities who have battled with drug addiction, such as Charlie Sheen or the late Whitney Houston, may have used similar justifications for their drug use. However, recognizing these patterns in thoughts and behaviors can help individuals avoid the same tragedies experienced by these public figures. Understanding that these types of thoughts and feelings are common among people struggling with substance dependency can be a valuable first step in seeking help and overcoming the addiction.

What Do You Think of When You Hear "Counseling?"

It's common to believe that a counselor holds the key to solving all our problems, but in reality, the solution lies within us. The client is the true expert on their own life and experiences, and holds the power to overcome their challenges. However, past experiences and emotional trauma may prevent them from recognizing this ability and seeking a path towards healing. A counselor can assist in guiding the individual towards self-discovery and unlocking their inner strength to find their own "silver bullet" solution.

Making and IMPACT

As a counselor, it is important to acknowledge that one does not possess the answer to every problem. Rather, a counselor's role is to provide support, offer a different perspective, and highlight the potential consequences of certain actions. The client is the expert in their own life, and holds the key to unlocking their own solutions. However, it is essential for a counselor to provide empathy and understanding to help the client reach their own solutions.

Being a counselor can be emotionally taxing, as one is exposed to the struggles and difficulties of others on a regular basis. It's crucial for counselors to engage in self-care activities to maintain their own well-being and effectively perform their role. This can help prevent burnout and ensure that they are able to continue providing support to their clients.

Life Outlook

The way we think about events in our lives has a significant impact on our emotions. Our Life Outlook, or attitude towards current events and situations, affects not only our present state but also our future. It influences our thoughts, feelings, decisions, and subsequent actions, which determine the consequences or results of those actions.

It's essential to understand that certain situations in life will inevitably lead to unpleasant emotions. However, it's crucial to consider how these emotions shape our Life Outlook. Will they perpetuate negative and destructive thoughts, or can they be redirected to generate a positive and productive outlook?

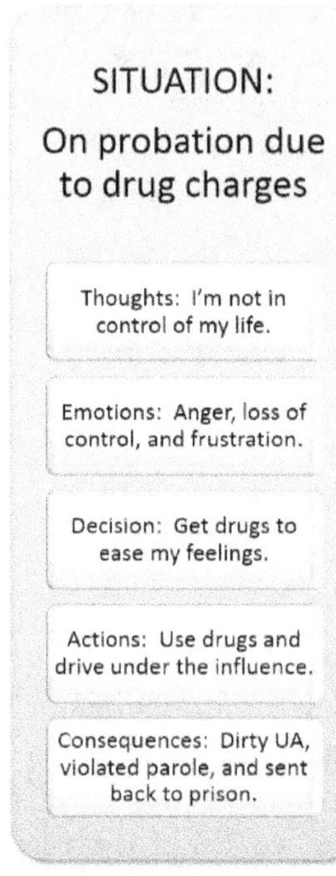

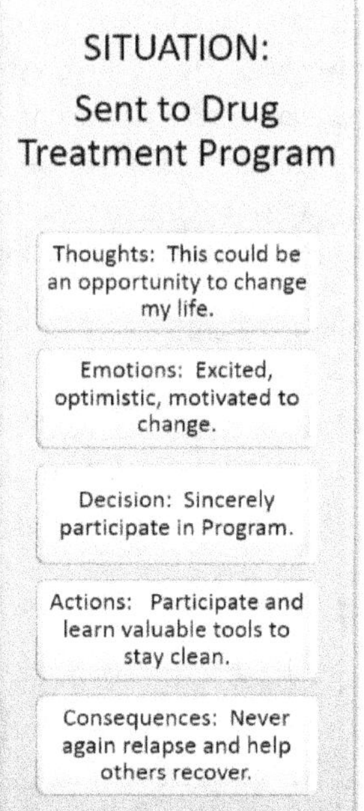

It's important to reflect on your personal Life Outlook and fill out the diagrams accordingly. Remember, a negative Life Outlook can lead to negative consequences, while a positive outlook can lead to positive results. Embracing the full range of emotions, including unpleasant ones, and redirecting them in a productive way can enhance the quality of your life.

Think of attitude as your potential – like a rock perched on a hill, ready to roll downhill. Attitude plays a significant role in shaping an individual's susceptibility to substance use. It is a multi-faceted concept that is shaped by a combination of genetic, environmental, and personal factors. The age-old debate of nature versus nurture is relevant in understanding the development of attitude, as genetics can make an individual predisposed to certain behaviors, while the environment and upbringing can steer the direction of these behaviors.

Attitude is the result of these factors, determining an individual's perceptions, thoughts, and emotions, which then influence decision-making and behavior, ultimately leading to the consequences of their actions. However, it is important to understand that attitude is not an unchangeable trait and can be altered. A change in attitude can result in a change in thoughts, feelings, and perceptions, thereby impacting behavior and leading to more favorable outcomes. What's your attitude in any situation?

<table>
<tr><td>SITUATION:
____
____

Thoughts:__________
____

Emotions:__________
____

Decision:__________
____

Actions:__________
____

Consequences: ______
__________</td><td>SITUATION:
____
____

Thoughts:__________
____

Emotions:__________
____

Decision:__________
____

Actions:__________
____

Consequences: ______
__________</td><td>SITUATION:
____
____

Thoughts:__________
____

Emotions:__________
____

Decision:__________
____

Actions:__________
____

Consequences: ______
__________</td></tr>
</table>

To alter one's attitude, it is necessary to first acknowledge the need for change and take the first step towards developing a different mindset. The process of changing attitude and substance use is a gradual and holistic one that addresses the root causes of the problem. The change begins with recognizing the need for change.

Male vs Female Attitude in Substance Use

The approach to drug use between men and women often varies as a result of differences in their coping mechanisms and self-perceptions. Men tend to attribute problems to external factors, such as blaming their boss if they lose their job or a ticket for a lack of clear signage. On the other hand, women often attribute problems to internal factors and see their actions as the root cause of negative outcomes, such as thinking they must have been performing poorly if they lose their job.

In drug treatment, it is crucial to address these differing attitudes and help both men and women recognize the influence of internal and external factors in their drug use. For men, this may involve encouraging introspection and taking responsibility for their actions. For women, it may involve emphasizing that not everything is their fault and teaching them to recognize and address the root causes of their drug use, such as depression or trauma.

It is also important to note that men and women may use drugs for different reasons. Women may turn to drugs as a coping mechanism for depression or traumatic events, while men may use drugs to escape the monotony of everyday life, to relax, to reward themselves, or to enhance their good times. Understanding these motivations can help inform more tailored and effective treatment approaches.

Step 7: Making Decisions

Based on our thoughts and emotions, we decide (also called "will" or volition) to perform an action, respond to a situation, or change a behavior. We must make a commitment to a specific course of action. Considering the long-term results will make the decision easier to make. Know what you are capable of accomplishing and set reasonable goals.

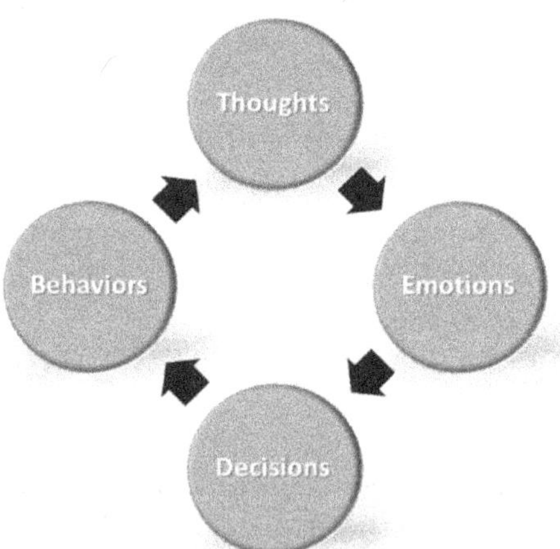

Our decisions, reactions, and behavior are influenced by our thoughts and emotions. Before deciding what action (if any), it's important to consider the consequences and weigh all options. It's best to take time to think about different solutions and how they may impact ourselves and those around us in the short and long term. Making a list of possible actions can also help us evaluate and choose the best solution. Keep in mind that quick decisions based on immediate pleasure may not lead to positive outcomes in the long run. It's essential to think carefully and consider the long-term effects of our actions.

Having a strong desire or willpower to change a behavior is a crucial first step, but it alone is not sufficient to bring about meaningful change. In order to effectively modify habits and actions, it is essential to have a thorough understanding of the steps necessary for transformation. According to McNulty (2009), individuals must have four key components in order to bring about lasting change:

1. Awareness of what needs to change

2. A clear understanding of the specific steps required to make the change

3. The capability to actually make the change, and

4. A strong desire to change.

Simply having a strong will is not enough if an individual lacks the knowledge and skills to implement the change. For example, a child might have a desire to drive a car, but without proper training and knowledge of how to operate a vehicle, they cannot do so safely. It is important to recognize one's limitations and set achievable goals in order to bring about successful and sustainable change.

The Reasoning Process

Not all decisions are rational. Some are led by emotions. Some are led by defense mechanisms. And sometimes we are just fooling ourselves. Let's examine reasons, excuses, and false motives for the decisions we make, so that we might be able to re-consider, be aware of our own thoughts, and make better decisions. This is essential if we are to improve our actions, and change our behaviors.

We truly are our own worst enemy. Given enough time, you can rationalize any excuse into a reason. According to the dictionary: A reason is a statement offered in explanation or justification, while an excuse is used to try to remove blame.

Normally a reason is associated with the correct justification behind an action and an excuse is just a false reason. Depending on which side of the fence you are on, you may be more accustomed to using excuses for explaining away mistakes, rather than biting the bullet and owning up to a mistake.

All of that is fine, but in the world of substance recovery, it is necessary for us to draw a definite line between the two. Addicts who want to continue to use drugs despite everyone else's best wishes for them will find excuses to go back to drug use. Recovering addicts who are experiencing ambivalence (simultaneous conflicting feelings about whether to quit using drugs or continue in their destructive behavior) can be manipulated by the addiction into thinking what they have is a reason to use drugs when it is really only an excuse.

- Client has no work experience

- Client gets out of jail

- Client applies for several jobs

- Client gets called back for an interview for one job

- Client does not get the job

- Client's self-talk "the world is against me and no one will ever give me a break"

- Client uses this as an excuse to return to drug use

When in reality very few people get the first job they apply for, imagine if every time you got turned down from a job you went on a two-week heroin spree. This situation actually has very little to do with the client not getting the job and more with the client's real desires. It goes back to rule #1 of R.O.A.R. It all goes back to that old cliché "found the right way to do the wrong thing."

False motives

Human beings give themselves permission to commit "bad" behavior if they can convince themselves or others that they are doing it for the right reason. For example, a client may justify robbing people because his family needs the money. He fails to mention that the reason his family needs the money is that he has spent all the money on drugs and has not worked in seven years. No one wants to have a bruised ego. Do not allow yourself to be fooled by false motives that stem from your addiction, "I am going to be the manager at a bar and not drink alcohol."

We judge ourselves based on our intentions, were as other people judge us based on our actions. Have a realistic, achievable recovery plan. A client might think, "My recovery is going to consist of me working seven twelve-hour shift, every day of the week." But this only leads to burnout. It is not realistic.

Acknowledge the significance of experiencing a little enjoyable, *drug-free* leisure activities. Adults often overlook the value of play, but children understand that play is a form of work. Adopting a childlike mindset towards play can bring numerous benefits. A constant work schedule, without breaks for leisure activities, is not a sustainable approach to recovery. This can lead to burnout, frustration, and ultimately, relapse. Hence, it's crucial to let loose sometimes, try new things, and have a little fun.

When working with clients, two relevant questions to ask are: (1) "What did you enjoy doing before drug use?" and (2) "What are five activities that you have never tried before and would like to experience for fun?" Often, drug use can lead to the neglect of previously enjoyed leisure activities such as playing catch, fishing, or taking a relaxing drive. If a client has limited experience with drug-free fun, question 2 can help them identify new activities they might enjoy. It's important to discuss if a coping skill brings up similar emotions as drug use and whether it addresses the root cause of drug use. The client is the expert in their life, and the goal is to find a healthy balance between work and play.

It's common for clients to feel the need to make up for lost time, but it's crucial to remember that lost time cannot be regained. Time is a finite resource, much like sand in an hourglass. Once the sand has fallen, it cannot be replaced. The inevitability of death gives life meaning and purpose.

Step 8: Take Action, Change Behaviors

The goal of treatment is to achieve positive, long-lasting behavioral changes through active therapeutic strategies. Our actions are determined by our thoughts, emotions, and will to change, and every individual has the freedom to make their own choices without being influenced by external factors or substances. While substances may appear to be the cause of certain actions, it is important to remember that the choice to use them always precedes the action.

Behaviors are the physical actions of the body. What individuals do with the body is determined by thoughts, emotions, and volition to change. We usually judge ourselves based on our motives or intentions, but others judge us based on our actions.

In daily life, it's common to come across individuals whose behavior seems inexplicable and causes us to question their actions. This internal dialogue can often lead to confusion and frustration, leaving us wondering why a person is acting the way they are. However, it's important to understand that every behavior has a purpose and a goal behind it. To better understand a person's behavior, we must first look at what they are trying to achieve with their actions. Whether it's a child throwing a tantrum in a grocery store or a colleague making an unexpected decision, all behavior is directed toward fulfilling a specific objective.

When we are able to recognize the goals behind a person's behavior, it helps us to understand their actions and motives better. This can be especially useful in improving our relationships with others, as it allows us to empathize with their situation and see things from their perspective. With this understanding, we are better equipped to respond to the situation in a more constructive way and find common ground. Ultimately, gaining insight into the reasons behind a person's behavior can help us to build stronger, more meaningful connections with those around us.

As a person continues to use drugs, they might experience temporary relief and euphoria, however, over time, the problems caused by drug use can accumulate and surpass the benefits it provides. This is a crucial turning point in drug addiction recovery, as it highlights the need to address the underlying issues rather than relying on drugs as a coping mechanism. It is important to recognize that drugs only provide temporary relief and do not address the root cause of the problem. In order to achieve lasting recovery, it is necessary to identify and work on resolving the underlying issues that led to drug use in the first place. This requires a dedicated and proactive approach, rather than relying on drugs as a quick fix.

In the beginning, the **Relief** from using substances outweighs the **Consequences**.

Over time, the **Consequences** become more severe and outweigh the temporary **Relief** of drug use.

In order to make positive and rewarding choices, it is crucial to consider the potential

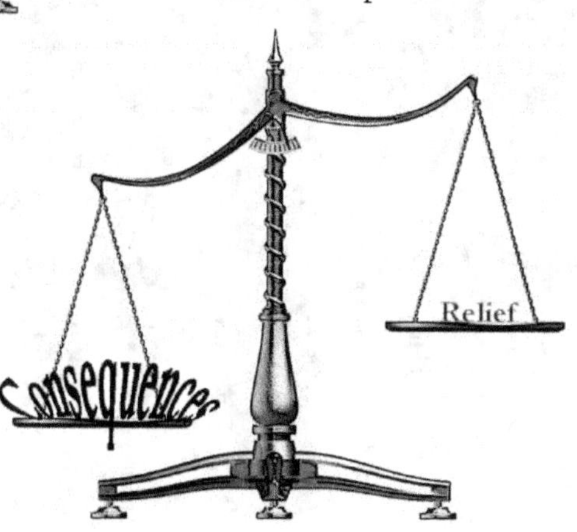

consequences and find pleasure in making the right decisions. Though the initial process of making good choices may cause temporary discomfort, persevering through these challenges will lead to successful behavior change and overcome cravings. Both ourselves and others judge us based on our actions, not our intentions.

Sobriety should be the top priority in recovery and should not be supplanted by anything else. Major life events, such as starting new relationships or working overtime, can increase stress levels and increase the risk of relapse. To minimize stress, it is recommended to limit work hours and avoid starting new relationships during recovery.

Family life can also be a source of stress, but focusing on recovery first will ultimately lead to easier management of family relationships. The key is to focus on recovery and let relationships naturally restore in due time. Restoring relationships is a high priority but remember, restoring relationships should not take priority over sobriety. Remember that **Recovery Restores Relationships.**

The Train Effect

1. I am standing on a train track.

2. The train is coming.

3. I turn my back to the train.

4. I close my eyes.

5. I put on headphones.

6. I do not hear or see the train.

7. The train is still coming.

The use of drugs may provide temporary relief from the problems one is facing, but it does not resolve the underlying issues. To effectively address substance abuse, it is important to identify the root cause, which can be referred to as the "train track." By recognizing the problem and taking the necessary steps to address it, individuals can overcome their dependence on drugs and begin to address the true needs in their life. Taking action is key, and the process of change requires a strong commitment and willingness to follow through with the necessary steps, even if they may be challenging at times. As the saying goes, "just do it," and trust in your ability to make positive changes in your life.

The Snowball Effect

The "snowball effect" occurs when someone starts using drugs in moderation, but gradually increases their usage as time goes on. The reason for this progression is rooted in the idea that if one dose yields the desired result, then more will only enhance the experience. This can often lead to full-blown relapse

and substance abuse. The progression of drug use might occur over an extended period, but it is a dangerous slope towards addiction, pain, or even death.

This cycle starts with the justification of "just one drink won't hurt" or "just one joint won't kill you". This initial success in using the substance with limited consequences builds trust and confidence in the individual's relationship with drugs. The individual might then increase their usage, repeating the cycle, until they eventually reach a point where their substance abuse becomes a problem.

Moreover, the cycle of substance abuse is often exacerbated by the false notion that drugs are the solution to the problems they are facing. However, in reality, drugs only serve to mask the problems and do not solve them. Substance abuse is a vicious cycle that can only be broken by recognizing the problem and taking the necessary steps towards change and recovery.

For instance, the client may argue that "I have a friend who drinks every weekend and still has a great job, a family and a good life. So, why can't I drink too?" He uses his friend's experience as a validation for his own drug use, but fails to see that everyone's journey with substance abuse is unique and what works for his friend may not work for him. By seeking external approval, the client tries to suppress his internal motives and rationalize his drug use. However, this only perpetuates the vicious cycle of addiction and the inevitable negative consequences that follow.

At the end of the client's evening, automatic associations have taken place and now the client feels as if he can "correctly" use alcohol. The success of drug use is the fuel to his fire. If you do drugs you will LOVE it. There is no coping skill in the world that compares to the crippling intensity of drugs.

What do you think is meant by "establishes trust in the relationship with the drug?" The phrase refers to the addict's perception that using the drug will consistently result in a positive outcome, such as relief from emotional or physical discomfort, or feelings of pleasure or euphoria. This reinforces the belief that the drug is a reliable source of comfort and pleasure, and the addict forms a trusting relationship with the substance. As a result, the likelihood of continued use and abuse increases, as the addict associates drug use with positive outcomes.

Making and IMPACT

What do you think is meant by "the success of his evening is the fuel to his fire?" It refers to the idea that the person's successful experience with drugs or alcohol is what reinforces their desire to continue using them. The initial successful use is seen as a positive experience and fuels the person's continued desire to use, creating a self-perpetuating cycle. This success can also contribute to building trust in the relationship with the drug, making the person more likely to use again in the future.

The occurrence of using drugs again, after a period of abstinence, is a common phenomenon in addiction. The initial act of indulging in drugs, even just once, can reignite the cravings and lead to a pattern of repeated drug use. The lack of immediate negative consequences only reinforces this behavior. This cycle is further exacerbated by one's ego, pride, or the desire to not feel defeated by anything or anyone, leading to a continuous pursuit of drug use. Addiction can be compared to a stray cat - once fed, it will keep coming back for more, and in this context, it is drugs. It is crucial to understand that the answer to avoiding addiction is not to try to find ways to use drugs responsibly, but rather to avoid using drugs altogether.

The Volcano

To effectively address drug addiction, it is crucial to understand the root cause behind the substance use. The underlying reason for starting drug use is often compared to an active volcano with the initial motive being the lava gradually rising to the surface, ready to erupt. Simply putting a cap on the volcano will not resolve the problem as the pressure will continue to build, manifesting itself in various forms such as uncontrolled overeating and weight gain (or excessive loss), uncontrollable pornography use, severe family conflicts, and loss of employment.

Therefore, it is imperative to identify the pressure that is driving the individual to seek refuge in drugs and what they hope to accomplish through substance use. By understanding the underlying motives and addressing them, the individual can find healthier coping mechanisms and prevent relapse.

So ask yourself, "What is my pressure point? What is it you are hoping to accomplish by using drugs?"

Step 9: Evaluate Consequences

Making and IMPACT

The process of decision-making in addressing substance abuse involves a thorough assessment of the potential outcomes associated with a chosen course of action. Outcomes can be interpreted as "consequences." This involves the consideration of both short and long-term effects, as actions and their resulting outcomes can bring forth both pleasure and pain. While the pleasure derived from drug use may be immediate, it may not outweigh the long-term adverse consequences. Interventions can aid individuals in objectively evaluating the potential outcomes and making informed decisions that promote lasting change.

Short-term consequences of drug use:

Impaired judgment and motor skills: Drug use affects the central nervous system, leading to impaired judgment, reaction time, and coordination. This can increase the risk of accidents, such as car crashes, falls, and drowning.

Increased risk of accidents and injuries: Drugs can impair the user's ability to make sound decisions, leading to increased risk of accidents and injuries. For example, a person under the influence of drugs may engage in dangerous activities, such as driving under the influence or participating in extreme sports.

Increased likelihood of engaging in risky behavior: Drug use can lead to an increased likelihood of engaging in high-risk activities such as unprotected sex, which can lead to sexually transmitted infections, or drug injection, which increases the risk of blood-borne infections.

Increased likelihood of overdose: Drugs affect the way the body functions, and in some cases, they can lead to an overdose. Consider how many famous stars have died from "accidental" overdoses, such as Elvis, Marylin Monroe, and Whitney Houston, just to mention a few. Overdosing on drugs can cause serious health problems and even death.

Decreased ability to perform daily tasks: Drug use can impair the user's ability to think clearly and perform daily tasks, leading to decreased productivity and difficulty with personal and professional responsibilities.

Changes in mood and behavior: Drug use can cause changes in mood, behavior, and personality. This can result in strained relationships with friends, family, and coworkers, as well as difficulties in maintaining personal and professional responsibilities.

Physical health problems: Drug use can cause a range of physical health problems, such as nausea, vomiting, headaches, and cardiovascular issues. Long-term drug use can also lead to chronic health problems and damage to internal organs.

Long-term consequences of drug use:

Addiction or dependence on the drug: Drug use can lead to addiction, which is a chronic, relapsing disorder characterized by compulsive drug seeking and use, despite the negative consequences. Addiction can lead to a physical dependence on the drug, which means the body has adjusted to the presence of the drug and requires it to function normally. Withdrawal symptoms can occur when drug use is stopped, and can be severe and even life-threatening.

Physical and mental health problems, including organ damage and cognitive decline: Drug use can cause physical and mental health problems, including organ damage, cognitive decline, and mental health disorders. For example, long-term drug use can cause damage to the liver, heart, and lungs, as well as brain damage and memory loss.

Increased risk of chronic illnesses: Drug use can increase the risk of chronic illnesses, such as liver disease, heart disease, and respiratory problems. These illnesses can have serious, long-term health consequences and may be life-threatening.

Financial problems due to the cost of the drug and decreased ability to work: Drug use can be expensive, leading to financial problems for the user and their loved ones. Additionally, drug use can impair the ability to work, leading to decreased income and difficulty meeting financial obligations.

Strained relationships with friends and family: Drug use can cause changes in mood and behavior, leading to strained relationships with friends and family. This can result in feelings of isolation and loneliness, and can have a significant impact on personal and professional relationships.

Legal problems, including arrests and incarceration: Drug use can lead to legal problems, including arrests for drug-related offenses and incarceration. The government might have the ability to acquire everything you purchased with drug money. You can lose everything. This can have serious consequences, including loss of employment and difficulty finding housing.

Homelessness and poverty: Drug use can lead to homelessness and poverty, as the financial and social consequences of drug use can have a significant impact on the individual's ability to maintain stable housing and employment. This can lead to a cycle of poverty, as the individual may struggle to meet basic needs, such as food, clothing, and shelter.

Finally, drug use can have far-reaching consequences, affecting the individual's physical, mental, and social well-being, as well as their relationships, finances, and legal status. The consequences of drug use can include addiction, physical and mental health problems, financial difficulties, strained relationships, legal problems, and even homelessness and poverty. Understand the impact of choices and be aware of the potential consequences of drug use. This requires an objective evaluation of the risks and benefits, and a consideration of the long-term impact of drug use on individuals and others.

Examining consequences will help individuals gain a clear understanding of the potential devastation and painful reality caused by continued drug use. This can involve education, counseling, and support to help individuals make informed decisions about drug use and their overall health and well-being. Through interventions, individuals can develop the skills and strategies they need to resist drug use and make lasting changes in their lives. Examining consequences will help individuals understand the impact of their choices and make decisions that promote their physical, mental, and social well-being. By recognizing the far-reaching consequences of drug use, individuals can take steps to protect their health, relationships, and overall quality of life.

Relapse Prevention

The Process of Relapse

Human behavior is not purely reactive to circumstances, but instead is the result of a deliberate thought process. This is particularly relevant when discussing the issue of relapse in recovery. Relapse is common, but not pre-determined. Being in recovery does not always lead to relapse. With caution and consistency, relapse might be avoided.

While it is widely accepted that relapse is a common occurrence, it is crucial to recognize the different types of triggers that can lead to a setback. These triggers can be broadly categorized into three categories: emotional, situational, and crisis. Each of these categories encompasses a range of unique stimuli that can result in relapse, including various emotions, environmental factors, and life-altering events. By being aware of the specific triggers that may impact one's recovery, individuals can take proactive steps to manage and mitigate these risks, leading to a more successful path towards lasting recovery.

Emotional triggers for drug relapse are often rooted in the desire to alter one's emotional state. Drugs can be used as a means of seeking relief from negative feelings or amplifying positive ones. Unfortunately, many individuals find themselves returning to drug use when they are faced with feelings they wish to change, often disregarding the potential consequences of their actions.

Situational triggers, on the other hand, arise from specific places or events that put an individual in a vulnerable position. These may involve lying to oneself or others about one's intentions, such as falsely promising not to drink at a social gathering. These triggers can be particularly dangerous, as individuals may be more likely to relapse due to a false sense of security.

Crisis triggers, which refer to intense and unexpected events that are difficult to handle, are another major contributor to relapse. These could include significant life events like the death of a loved one or a significant fight with a partner. Individuals may be particularly vulnerable to relapse during these events, as they may feel overwhelmed and unable to cope with the emotions they are facing.

It's not accurate to assume that people simply react to situations without conscious thought. Our perception can play a significant role in preventing relapse triggers. For instance, when a male addict sees a beer commercial with a seductive woman, he can choose to view it as a trigger for relapse or as a reminder of the negative consequences that resulted from his alcohol consumption.

Relapse often starts with fond memories of substance use and can be triggered by the romanticization of past experiences. To counteract this, it's important to remember the significant consequences of substance use and to keep those consequences at the forefront of our minds. This can be done through creating a wallet card or placing a reminder in a visible location, such as on the inside of a doorframe.

As time passes, the consequences of substance use may appear less severe. It's important to continuously remind ourselves of what we have learned in the past and how we do not want to repeat past mistakes.

Additionally, it's a common misconception that being a man means being able to handle everything on one's own. Even being a Christian does not mean you can handle everything on your own. "I can do all things THROUGH CHRIST who strengthens me," (Philippians 4:13 KJV) means that Christ is the One who is strong, and He will be our strength when we rely on Him in all situations. True strength lies in acknowledging and seeking help when necessary. Crying is not a sign of weakness, and being a man does not equate to always knowing the right thing or making the right decision. This is why the apostle Paul said "When I am weak, then I am strong." Because God was his strength. And again, the Lord told Paul, "My grace is sufficient for you, for my power is made perfect in weakness." (2 Cor. 12:9).

Most Common Relapse Thoughts

"It's legal."

The statement, "It's legal," refers to the legality of certain substances, particularly alcohol and tobacco. While these drugs are legal, they are also incredibly dangerous and can serve as a gateway to other, more harmful substances. It is important to recognize that just because a substance is legal does not mean it is safe or without consequences. The idea that "my problem was with X drug, not alcohol" is a common justification for drinking, but it is important to remember that alcohol is a drug and its use can have severe consequences. Just because someone may drink without consequences does not mean that the same will be true for everyone. Addicts should not look to others for justification for their own behavior, but rather take responsibility for their actions and the consequences that result from them.

"It's just a little bit."

The notion of "a little bit of drug use" is an illusion and a dangerous justification for the start of addiction. There is no such thing as a limited amount when it comes to harmful substances and the toll they can take on a person's life. The temporary pleasure obtained from drug use is not worth sacrificing long-term health and well-being.

As for the idea of "hanging out with old friends," it's important to evaluate the nature of these relationships and determine if they are truly supportive. The individuals who claim to be friends but only provide support in exchange for drugs do not deserve to be considered true friends. It's crucial to distinguish between genuine friends and acquaintances and prioritize relationships that bring positive influences and support into one's life.

"I'm bored."

Managing monotony can be challenging, especially when daily routines don't provide enough stimulation or fulfillment. For someone in recovery, finding a healthy balance between work and leisure is crucial. Overworking or becoming too sedentary can hinder progress in recovery. It is important to encourage clients to explore new experiences and activities that boost their self-esteem, self-efficacy, and sense of empowerment. This could include outdoor activities such as hiking, participating in community events like high school sports games, or building new relationships or rekindling old ones with supportive, clean, and sober family and friends. Community involvement and volunteering can also provide a sense of purpose and improve community awareness. Additionally, it is important to note that coping skills are not permanent solutions, and it is normal for them to evolve and change as their effectiveness decreases over time.

"FORGET IT!"

Supporting someone who has given up on their recovery journey can be a delicate task, but it is crucial to approach it with compassion and understanding. The first step in offering support is to validate their feelings. Listen to their frustrations and acknowledge their emotions without judgment. This can help the client feel heard and understood.

Sharing your own experiences can also be helpful. If you have faced similar challenges in your recovery journey, share your story and how you overcame them. This can help the client feel less isolated and more motivated. Reassuring the client that the feelings of hopelessness they are experiencing are temporary can also help them to see the light at the end of the tunnel.

It's essential to address the root cause of the client's crisis and work together to find a solution. Discuss the long-term consequences of relapse and emphasize that the guilt and shame of relapsing is not worth it. Reframe relapse as not being a necessary part of recovery and encourage the client to stay committed to their journey. Create a supportive and non-judgmental environment that helps the client navigate through this difficult time and overcome their challenges.

Relapse is **not** an inevitable aspect of the recovery process. The belief that relapse is a normal part of recovery can arise from an individual trying to alleviate feelings of guilt and shame associated with drug use. However, these feelings of guilt and shame serve as an important reminder of the consequences of drug use and are necessary for maintaining motivation towards sobriety. Do not to fall into the trap of believing that relapse is a necessary step in recovery, as this can lead to a relapse and a return to addiction. Remain focused. Sober. Committed to the recovery journey.

Stages of Relapse

Relapse Stage 1 – Looking for Excuses

- Misleading Intentions: Refers to actions or decisions that are driven by an ulterior or hidden motive, rather than genuine or honest intentions.

- Obtaining and Implementing Consent Declarations: Refers to the process of obtaining explicit consent or agreement from individuals or parties before proceeding with a particular action or decision.

- Engaging in Cognitive Distortions: Refers to the tendency to perceive and interpret information in a way that is biased or inaccurate, leading to irrational or flawed thinking patterns.

- Impediments to Effective Thinking: Refers to obstacles or barriers that prevent one from thinking critically, logically, and rationally, leading to negative consequences and outcomes.

- Excuse Making: Refers to the act of offering excuses or explanations for one's behavior, even when they are unreasonable or invalid, in order to justify one's actions.

- Underestimating the Severity of a Situation: Refers to the tendency to minimize or downplay the negative impact or consequences of a situation, even when they are significant.

- Justifying Irrational Behaviors: Refers to the process of offering explanations or reasons for behaviors that are not logically or morally justifiable, in order to make them appear more reasonable or acceptable.

Some of the terminology in "Stage 1: Looking for Excuses" may appear to be foreign. We judge ourselves based on our intentions and others judge us based on our actions. What do this mean and how does it pertain to recovery? Well I might lie to myself and others by saying things like "I'm going to the bar to watch the game." This is an example of a false motive. All along I planned on going to the bar to drink beer. However, this was not a socially acceptable excuse and people would think poorly of me if I told them my real intentions.

Permission Statements are things that we tell ourselves to make our negative behavior ok to ourselves. No one wants to be perceives as a bad person. Therefore I might tell myself something like "I'm just going to do [it] this once and its ok because weed is not a big deal."

Jeffery makes really bad decisions while on Xanax and crack cocaine. He has suffered a lot of consequences as a result of these drugs. He realized this and upon completion of his last treatment program voiced that he "is not going to use Xanax, but he is going to smoke weed from time-to-time." He never identified the marijuana as a problem because he would normally experience "successful drug use" while using cannabis.

What do you think is meant by the terminology of "successful drug use?" This means that people were able to use this drug, receive the relief or effects, and experience minimal consequences. However, cannabis was the gateway drug and the "successful" use of the drug was the accelerant to the fire that lead to his eventual progression to Xanax. The solution to the problem was not to use marijuana.

Tobacco as a Gateway Drug

- Get out of prison
- Smoke cigarettes
- Get a buzz
- Reward yourself with cigarettes at every opportunity
- No more buzz from the cigarettes
- "If I can smoke cigarettes, then I can drink beer"
- Smoke cigarettes and drink only a few beers
- This pattern continues for x amount of time
- Frequency of alcohol use increases
- One day while drunk and smoking cigarettes someone pulls out marijuana

- You justify that marijuana is very similar, and just another kind of tobacco.
- Initial marijuana use.

Alcohol as a Gateway Drug

- Secretly romanticizing the idea of using alcohol
- Begins to go to the bar to "watch the game" (false motive)
- Goes to the bar regularly
- Eventually gives in because his team won and he "had" to drink a beer
- Frequency of alcohol use increases
- Runs into an old friend on the way home from a bar
- Normally would of said no, however under the influence of alcohol.
- Gives in and begins to use meth again

People have a tendency to believe that a process takes a long time. For example, the tobacco situation where the person progressed back to his drug of choice in approximately 2 years. This progression took place just in a few months.

Relapse Stage 2 – Socially Acceptable Drugs

Socially acceptable drugs refer to substances that are widely used, accepted, or sanctioned within a particular culture, community, or society. These drugs can include prescription medications, over-the-counter remedies, alcohol, tobacco, and even caffeine. And in many states, now marijuana is socially acceptable. These are also referred to as "gateway drugs."

Despite their widespread use and acceptance, these drugs can pose significant health and safety risks, as they have the potential to cause dependence, overdose, or other harmful effects when consumed in excessive or inappropriate quantities. For example, prescription painkillers can be highly addictive and have led to the opioid epidemic in the United

Making and IMPACT

States. Now less serious drugs like marijuana are unknowingly being laced with deadly drugs like fentanyl. Meanwhile alcohol use (which is legal) can cause serious liver damage, brain damage, and other health issues, including death.

Moreover, the social stigma attached to the use of certain drugs may lead individuals to underestimate the dangers associated with these substances, leading to risky or harmful behavior. In addition, the availability and accessibility of these drugs can increase the likelihood of abuse and misuse, as well as the risk of negative consequences for both the user and those around them.

Socially acceptable drugs, despite their widespread use and cultural acceptance, can pose serious health and safety risks and should be used with caution and in accordance with appropriate guidelines and recommendations.

Relapse Stage 3 – Progression to Drug of Choice

Moving from socially acceptable drugs to hard drugs refers to the progression or escalation of drug use from less harmful or more socially acceptable substances to more dangerous or illicit drugs. This progression is often seen as a slippery slope, as individuals may start with experimenting with drugs that are perceived as harmless or socially acceptable, before moving on to harder drugs with more severe consequences.

The transition from socially acceptable drugs to hard drugs can be driven by a variety of factors, including increased tolerance, dependence, or addiction to the initial drug of use, peer pressure, or the pursuit of a more intense or satisfying high. Additionally, the availability, accessibility, and affordability of hard drugs may also contribute to the progression of drug use.

It is important to note that this progression is not inevitable, and individuals can make the choice to stop using drugs before they move on to more dangerous or addictive substances. However, for those who have already made this transition, it can be challenging to overcome addiction and break the cycle of drug abuse, and may require professional treatment and support.

The progression from socially acceptable drugs to hard drugs is a complex and multi-faceted issue that is driven by a range of social, psychological, and behavioral factors. Addressing this issue requires a comprehensive and integrated approach that considers individual, community, and societal factors, and provides support and resources for individuals who are struggling with addiction and substance abuse.

158

Understanding the Stages of Change

Substance Use Disorder (SUD) is a chronic and potentially relapsing condition that necessitates substantial perseverance and commitment to overcome. The process of change can be long and difficult, however, it is achievable. The beginning of the change process lies with the individual user's decision to begin. While the support and encouragement of others can play a pivotal role, ultimately, it is a personal decision. The stages of change advance from pre-contemplation to a lifelong commitment to maintaining sobriety.

Stage 1: Pre-contemplation

Pre-contemplation is the first stage of change regarding substance use, and it is characterized by a lack of awareness or motivation to change one's behavior. During this stage, an individual may not see their substance use as a problem, or they may be unaware of the negative consequences of their behavior. They may be resistant to change, or they may not have the information they need to make an informed decision.

Individuals in the pre-contemplation stage may be in denial about their substance use or may minimize the impact it has on their lives. They may make excuses for their behavior or blame others for their problems. They may also feel a sense of shame or stigma associated with substance use, which can make it difficult to acknowledge that they have a problem.

It is common for individuals to remain in the pre-contemplation stage for a long time, as they may not be ready or willing to change. It is important to note that forcing someone to change before they are ready is often counterproductive and can lead to resistance or resentment.

There are a few ways to help individuals move out of the pre-contemplation stage and towards change. One effective approach is to provide education and information about substance use and its negative consequences. This can help individuals see the impact their behavior is having on their lives and increase their motivation to change.

Another approach is to engage in motivational interviewing, a client-centered counseling approach that aims to help individuals explore their ambivalence about change and increase their motivation to change. During this process, a trained professional listens actively to the individual, helps them to explore their values, goals, and concerns, and supports them in making a decision about change.

The pre-contemplation stage is an important part of the change process and requires a non-judgmental and supportive approach. By providing education and information and engaging in motivational interviewing, individuals may become more aware of the impact of their substance use and more motivated to change. However, it is important to note that change is a personal decision, and you can't force someone to change. Individuals may need to move through the other stages of change before they are ready to take action.

Stage 2: Contemplation

Contemplation is the second stage of change regarding substance use, and it is characterized by ambivalence and uncertainty about changing one's behavior. During this stage, an individual is aware of the negative consequences of their substance use but is not yet committed to change. They may be weighing the pros and cons of continuing to use substances versus quitting and considering the impact of their behavior on their relationships, career, health, and overall quality of life.

Contemplation can be a difficult stage for individuals to move through, as they may experience conflicting feelings and thoughts. They may want to change but feel uncertain about their ability to do so, or they may be afraid of what life will be like without substance use. They may also feel a sense of loss or mourning for the role that substance use has played in their life.

One way to help individuals move out of the contemplation stage is to provide support and encouragement while acknowledging their ambivalence. This can involve helping them to explore their values, goals, and concerns, and supporting them in making a decision about change.

Motivational interviewing can be a useful approach during this stage, as it allows individuals to explore their ambivalence in a safe and non-judgmental environment.

Another approach is to help individuals to identify and challenge any barriers or obstacles that may be preventing them from changing. These may include fear of withdrawal symptoms, concerns about how they will cope with stress or negative emotions, or lack of social support. By addressing these barriers, individuals may be more likely to move towards change.

It is important to note that individuals may remain in the contemplation stage for an extended period, and it is important to support them without pushing them to change before they are ready. This stage of change is necessary but rushing or pressuring someone to change can be counterproductive and may result in resistance or reluctance to move forward. Change occurs only when the individual decides to change.

Stage 3: Preparation

Preparation is the third stage of change regarding substance use, and it is characterized by a commitment to change and the initiation of specific steps to prepare for change. During this stage, an individual has made the decision to change and is taking concrete steps to prepare for that change. This stage is critical for success, as it sets the stage for the actual change to occur.

Individuals in the preparation stage may begin by seeking out information about treatment options and support programs, such as detoxification programs, residential treatment centers, outpatient treatment, and support groups. They may also begin to talk to friends and family members about their decision to change and to seek out support from those who are willing and able to provide it.

Preparing for change may also involve making changes to the environment to reduce triggers for substance use. This can involve removing drugs and alcohol from the home, avoiding places or people associated with substance use, and finding alternative activities to engage in that support sobriety.

Another important aspect of the preparation stage is setting specific goals and creating a plan to achieve those goals. This may involve identifying specific behaviors that need to be changed, such as developing healthier coping mechanisms, managing stress in a new way, or improving communication with loved ones. Creating a plan with specific steps to achieve these goals can help individuals stay on track and feel a sense of progress and accomplishment.

During this stage, individuals may also begin to address any co-occurring mental health disorders, such as depression, anxiety, or PTSD, that may be contributing to their substance use. This can involve seeking out mental health treatment, medication, or therapy to help manage these conditions and support sobriety.

It is important to note that the preparation stage can be challenging and may involve setbacks and obstacles. However, by staying committed to the goal of change and seeking out support and resources, individuals can move towards the action stage and take concrete steps to achieve sobriety.

The preparation stage is an important part of the change process and involves commitment, planning, and action. By seeking out information, support, and resources, individuals can set specific goals and create a plan to achieve those goals. This can help them stay on track and feel a sense of progress and accomplishment, which can be motivating as they move towards the action stage.

Stage 4: Action

Action is the fourth stage of change regarding substance use, and it is characterized by taking concrete steps to change one's behavior. During this stage, an individual has begun to make changes to their behavior and is actively working to achieve sobriety. This stage is often the most challenging, as individuals may face withdrawal symptoms, cravings, and a host of other challenges.

In the action stage, individuals may participate in a treatment program, attend support groups, or implement lifestyle changes to support sobriety. Treatment programs can vary in intensity and duration, and may involve inpatient or outpatient care. Support groups, such as Alcoholics Anonymous or Narcotics Anonymous, can provide ongoing support and a sense of community for individuals in recovery.

Lifestyle changes can also be a critical part of the action stage. These may include changes to diet and exercise, the development of new hobbies or interests, and the adoption of healthy coping mechanisms. It is important to note that these changes may take time and effort to develop, and it is essential to stay committed to the goal of sobriety.

During the action stage, individuals may also need to address any underlying psychological or emotional issues that may be contributing to their substance use. This can involve participating in individual or group therapy, practicing mindfulness techniques, or learning new ways to manage stress and negative emotions.

It is important to have a support system in place during the action stage, as individuals may experience setbacks and challenges. A strong support system can provide encouragement, accountability, and practical support as individuals navigate the difficulties of the recovery process.

The action stage is a critical part of the change process and requires dedication and perseverance. By participating in treatment programs, attending support groups, implementing lifestyle changes, and addressing underlying psychological and emotional issues, individuals can take concrete steps to achieve sobriety. However, it is important to remember that the recovery process is ongoing, and individuals may need to continue working on maintaining their sobriety for an extended period.

Stage 5: Maintenance

Maintenance is the fifth and final stage of change regarding substance use, and it is characterized by ongoing efforts to maintain sobriety and prevent relapse. During this stage, an individual has successfully made changes to their behavior and is working to sustain their sobriety over the long term.

Maintaining sobriety can be challenging, and it often requires ongoing effort and vigilance. Individuals in the maintenance stage may continue to participate in treatment programs and support groups, as well as implement lifestyle changes to support their recovery. They may also develop new coping mechanisms to manage stress and negative emotions and may focus on building healthy relationships and social support networks.

In the maintenance stage, individuals may also need to develop strategies to prevent relapse. This can involve identifying and avoiding triggers for substance use, such as certain people, places, or activities, as well as learning to manage cravings and urges. Individuals may also need to develop a relapse prevention plan that outlines steps to take in the event of a relapse and includes contact information for support and treatment resources.

It is important to note that the maintenance stage can be challenging, and individuals may experience setbacks and relapses. It is essential to stay committed to the goal of sobriety and to seek out support and resources when needed. Individuals may also benefit from working with a therapist or counselor to address any ongoing psychological or emotional issues that may be impacting their recovery.

Celebrating successes and milestones can also be an important part of the maintenance stage. This can help individuals stay motivated and feel a sense of progress and accomplishment. It can also be helpful to reflect on the positive changes that have occurred as a result of sobriety, such as improved relationships, better physical health, and a greater sense of purpose and meaning in life.

In conclusion, the maintenance stage is a critical part of the change process and requires ongoing effort and commitment. But again, Change occurs only when the individual decides to change. By continuing to participate in treatment programs, attending support groups, implementing lifestyle changes, and developing strategies to prevent relapse, individuals can sustain their sobriety over the long term. However, remember that the recovery process is ongoing, and individuals may need to continue working on maintaining their sobriety for the rest of their lives.

The stages of change for SUDs is a critical framework for understanding the process of recovery. Each stage presents its unique challenges, and success requires dedication and support from both the individual and their support network. By progressing through these stages, individuals can achieve and maintain sobriety, leading to a healthier and more fulfilling life.

Conclusion

Recovery from drug addiction requires a deeper understanding of the reasons behind drug use and the consequences that come with it. At first, drugs may appear to be a solution to life's problems, offering temporary pleasure and relief from stress. However, with continued use, the negative impacts such as physical harm, legal issues, and even death, will eventually outweigh the short-term euphoria.

For those struggling with drug addiction, life itself can be overwhelming. The everyday ups and downs of emotions can be difficult to navigate, particularly for those who have not learned how to live life on life's terms. It is important to understand that even in sobriety, life will still present challenges and frustrations. The choice lies with the individual to either accept these frustrations as a normal part of life or use them as an excuse to return to drug use.

Ultimately, the long-term consequences of drug use will outweigh any short-term relief experienced. Overcoming addiction requires recognizing this and seeking support from loved ones, friends, and professional counselors. By working together, individuals can break free from drug dependence and build a healthier and more fulfilling future.

What Do You Want Out of Recovery?

As a client, you have the ultimate authority and control over your life. It is only logical that you have the responsibility to decide what you desire to achieve through your recovery journey. The choice is yours to make. Would you like to limit yourself to consuming a maximum of two or three beers every night? Would you prefer to limit your drug use to just one joint per night? Or, would you rather remain completely abstinent from drugs?

Making and IMPACT

Ultimately, the decision is yours and it is essential that you make a decision that aligns with your personal goals and values.

The choice of whether to use tobacco during recovery is an important decision to consider. Tobacco, like any other drug, affects the way a person feels and reinforces the habit of using a substance to cope with life. Instead of simply switching from one addiction to another, it is important to strive for a healthier change and ultimately break the addictive cycle altogether. While it may be tempting to replace the use of "hard" drugs with tobacco or alcohol, research suggests that these substances can actually serve as gateway drugs and perpetuate the addictive lifestyle. The ultimate goal for those seeking recovery should be to move towards a lifestyle free from addictive behaviors, as the possibility of being addiction-free does exist.

The Choices

1. Do you want to replace one addiction with another?

2. Do you want to stop the addictive lifestyle all together?

Choice #2 is possible; however, it is no easy task. This choice is only recommended for people who are serious about changing their lives.

It's crucial to understand why individuals turn to drugs as a means of coping with life's challenges. While drugs may temporarily alleviate emotional discomfort or physical pain, they do not directly address or resolve the underlying issues. In fact, drug use may only serve as a temporary numbing of the senses, leading to an avoidance or inhibition of problem-solving in the future. It's important to acknowledge that relying on drugs to escape one's problems only perpetuates the cycle of addiction and hinders one's ability to effectively address and overcome their challenges. Ultimately, it's vital to critically evaluate the role drugs play in one's life and consider alternative, healthier coping mechanisms to address and resolve life's difficulties.

It's Not as Easy as Just Saying "No"

As much as we all loved President Ronald Reagan, the slogan "Just Say No" created and championed by Nancy was also "Just So Wrong." It may have been catchy, but it was too naïve and simplistic. Many clients within the criminal justice system hold the belief that simply making a decision to abstain from drug use is enough to achieve sobriety. However, it is crucial to understand the extent to which drugs and drug use have permeated various aspects of one's life. This includes experiencing negative consequences as a result of drug use, damage to primary relationships, limiting one's social circle to facilitate drug use, and the amount of time and energy dedicated to obtaining and using drugs. Without acknowledging these factors, it becomes difficult to fully grasp the challenge of overcoming drug addiction and make a successful transition towards a drug-free life.

The choice between valuing one's behavior or one's friends can greatly impact a person's decision to continue drug use or not. If a person's friends do not approve of their drug use, they may alter their behavior, hide their behavior, or seek out new friends who are more accepting of their actions. Often, individuals who struggle with drug addiction will opt for secret drug use or form new relationships with people who condone their negative behavior.

In order to make a successful transition into a drug-free lifestyle, it's important to reevaluate and reshape the social circle. This includes being mindful of the kind of friends who are supportive and encourage positive decision making. Friends who discourage sobriety or make light of harmful behavior are not truly supportive and should not be considered true friends.

Breaking away from drug use involves a transformation of one's life, and it's crucial to set strong boundaries to safeguard against those who still engage in drug use and negative behavior. People close to you may resist your change, but it's essential to remain steadfast and confident in your decision to live a drug-free life. At the end of the day, friends who are unhappy with your decision to pursue sobriety are not truly concerned about your long-term well-being. Who do you see as a problem?

The Mask of Drugs and Alcohol

When dealing with substance use disorder, it's crucial to be honest with oneself and recognize the underlying reasons for drug use. Substance use is a fatal progression. Initially, drugs may provide a temporary escape from problems, offering a sense of pleasure and stress relief. However, as time goes by, continued drug use can lead to harmful physical effects, legal consequences, and even death, making the euphoric feeling no longer worth the risk.

The allure of drugs can create a facade that masks the realities of life, tempting individuals to avoid taking responsibility and facing challenges. However, this only perpetuates the cycle of addiction, hindering personal growth and development. To break free from the grip of addiction, it's essential to acknowledge the negative impact of drugs on life and take a conscious effort to overcome their influence.

It's important to understand that drug use provides only a temporary escape from life's difficulties, preventing individuals from confronting their problems and learning how to cope with them effectively. By seeking support from loved ones and professionals, and depending on the Lord, individuals can embrace the challenges of recovery and work towards a healthier, more fulfilling future free from the "mask of drugs." It's vital to have faith in Lord as well as the process of change, because recovery requires dedication and commitment. The rewards of a drug-free life are well worth the effort.

BIBLIOGRAPHY

Alcoholics Anonymous big book: Including : Personal stories for the year 2008 (Special ed.). (2007). Place of publication not identified: AA.

Association for Psychological Science. (2011, January 25). People aren't born afraid of spiders and snakes: Fear is quickly learned during infancy. *ScienceDaily*. Retrieved February 20, 2023 from www.sciencedaily.com/releases/2011/01/110124111144.htm

Baumeister, R. F., Campbell, J. D., Krueger, J. I., & Vohs, K. D. (2003). Does high self-esteem cause better performance, interpersonal success, happiness, or healthier lifestyles? Psychological Science in the Public Interest, 4(1), 1-44.

Brehm, J., & Cohen, A. (1962). Explorations in cognitive dissonance. New York: Wiley.

Drug. (n.d.). Retrieved December 24, 2015, from http://www.merriam-webster.com/dictionary/drug

Dryden, W. (2011). The "ABCs" of REBT i: A preliminary study of errors and confusions in counselling and psychotherapy textbooks. Journal of Rational-Emotive & Cognitive-Behavior Therapy, pages 1-40.

Ego. (n.d.). Retrieved January 21, 2023, from http://www.merriam-webster.com/dictionary/ego

Janusik, L. (2007). Building Listening Theory: The Validation of the Conversational Listening Span. Communication Studies, 139-156.

Kirmayer, L. (1990). Resistance, Reactance, and Reluctance to Change: A Cognitive Attributional Approach to Strategic Interventions. Journal of Cognitive Psychotherapy, 4(2).

Logan, T., Walker, R., Cole, J., & Leukefeld, C. (2004). Victimization and substance abuse among women: Contributing factors, interventions, and implications. Review of General Psychology, 325-397.

Marvin, D. (1997). The Dynamics of Domestic Abuse. PsycEXTRA Dataset.

Maslow, A., & Stephens, D. (2000). The Maslow business reader. New York: Wiley.

Massie, H., & Szajnberg, N. (2006). My life is a longing: Child abuse and its adult sequelae Results of the Brody longitudinal study from birth to age 30. International Journal of Psychoanalysis, 472-496.

McMurran, M. (n.d.). Alcohol and violence. Child Abuse Rev. Child Abuse Review, 219-230.

McNulty, T. (2009). Demanding the Impossible: Desire and Social Change. Differences, 1-39.

National Center for Statistics and Analysis. (2014, December). Alcohol impaired driving: 2013 data. (Traffic Safety Facts. DOT HS 812 102). Washington, DC: National Highway Traffic Safety Administration.

Olds, J., & P. Milner. (1954). "Positive reinforcement produced by electrical stimulation of septal area and other regions of rat brain." *Journal of Comparative and Physiological Psychology* 47:419–27.

Palombo, J. (2013). The Self As a Complex Adaptive System Part II: Levels of Analysis and the Position of the Observer. Psychoanal. Soc. Work, 20:115-133.

Rodriguez, C. (2006). Attributional Style as a Mediator Between Parental Abuse Risk and Child Internalizing Symptomatology. Child Maltreatment, 121-130.

ABOUT THE AUTHOR

Doyle O. Welborn, is an experienced professional in the field of psychology, with over 15 years of practical experience working with incarcerated individuals in the state of Texas. Welborn holds a Master of Science degree in Psychology and is a Licensed Chemical Dependency Counselor who has dedicated much of his career to understanding the effects of substance use and addiction.

As a practitioner in the prison system, Welborn has worked with a diverse range of clients struggling with substance use issues. He has facilitated both large and individual group sessions to address the root causes of addiction, and has documented effective methods for promoting change.

One of the critical populations that Welborn has worked with is incarcerated individuals who are enrolled in substance use treatment programs. Through his work with these clients, he has helped them to reintegrate into society as sober and productive members. This has been achieved through a combination of evidence-based interventions, including counseling, behavioral therapy, and medication-assisted treatment.

Welborn's experience highlights the importance of addressing substance use issues within the context of a comprehensive treatment program that includes both individual and group therapy sessions. His work has demonstrated that effective substance use treatment must address the root causes of addiction, including psychological and environmental factors.

The success of Welborn's approach is evidenced by the positive outcomes achieved by his clients. By addressing the underlying problems that contribute to addiction, his clients are better equipped to manage and regulate their emotions and behaviors, and successfully reintegrate into society as sober and productive members, enabling them to live healthier, more fulfilling lives.